WIDE CROSSING

Wide Crossing

The West Africa Rice Development Association in transition, 1985-2000

JOHN R. WALSH

Routledge
Taylor & Francis Group
LONDON AND NEW YORK

First published 2001 by Ashgate Publishing

2 Park Square, Milton Park, Abingdon, Oxon OX14 4RN
605 Third Avenue, New York, NY 10017

Routledge is an imprint of the Taylor & Francis Group, an informa business

First issued in paperback 2021

A Library of Congress record exists under LC control number: 2001089781

ISBN 13: 978-1-138-72188-3 (hbk)
ISBN 13: 978-0-367-24961-8 (pbk)

Contents

Preface

My interest in the West Africa Rice Development Association dates from early 1985 when I visited the WARDA field office in St. Louis, Senegal at the mouth of the Senegal River. WARDA was on the itinerary because of its capabilities in research on rice. The rising popularity of rice as a staple food in West Africa and the failure of domestic rice production to meet demand had resulted in the heavy importation of rice. This was a main factor in the balance-of-payments problem plaguing Senegal and other countries in the region.

The application of modern agricultural techniques and technology to rice cultivation was seen as the best hope for improving yields in a key crop in the region. I was on my way upriver to visit irrigated rice perimeters around the village of Bakel in the middle valley of the Senegal where such innovation was being attempted. The projects, underwritten by American and European donor agencies, were designed to help farmers increase production of rice and make it possible for West African country to reduce rice imports.

At the time, a major dam construction project on the Senegal River was nearing completion. The project was intended to promote development of the river valley; a central objective was to control the flow of the river to benefit irrigated agriculture, particularly cultivation of rice. A main drawback was that the rice varieties being used produced poor yields even under irrigated conditions. Much the same was true in wetter areas of West Africa where farmers depended on rainfall in growing their rice crops. The varieties being planted along the Senegal were mostly imported from Asia and had proved vulnerable to the climate, pests and plant diseases of West Africa. The effects of drought in 1983-84 in the Sahel added urgency to the quest for more productive rice types.

Much depended on WARDA and other agricultural research organizations being able to develop high-yielding varieties of rice that would flourish in the region and help justify expenditures on the dams. In the middle 1980s, however, WARDA was experiencing internal and external difficulties that put its existence in question and certainly made it unlikely that it could achieve the research goals set for it.

WARDA did endure and the following account of the changes it underwent had its origins in a casual conversation in 1995 with the center's research director, Peter Matlon, and a later exchange with its director general, Eugene Terry. What we discussed was the idea of an account of WARDA's recent history in a style less formal than that of regular WARDA publications and that would portray the interplay of science, economics and politics that characterize the operations of international agricultural research centers like WARDA. Important and frequently left out of such discussions are the realities of living and working in a developing country in postcolonial Africa. The upshot was an invitation that enabled me to spend about three weeks in the summer of 1996 at the WARDA headquarters and research station at Bouaké, Côte d'Ivoire. I was given full access to staff at every level and was free to observe the functioning of the center, and with no strings attached.

I am grateful to Eugene Terry for making this venture possible and to him and to Peter Matlon for their patience and candor throughout our lengthy conversations about WARDA both in Bouaké and in the United States after they had completed their time at the center. I am indebted to the late David Bell, last of Harvard, for his insight into the early times and troubles of WARDA as I am for his giving me the benefit of his perspective over the years on international development matters. I am obliged to WARDA's current director general, Kanayo Nwanze, for going out of his way to bring me up to date on WARDA and for permission to use WARDA material as illustrations.

I owe my understanding of WARDA and how it works to interviews in Côte d'Ivoire and the United States. Errors of fact or interpretation are entirely my own. In Washington, early discussions with Gordon MacNeil set me off in the right direction, and, later, Curt Farrar, Dana Dalrymple, Alex McCalla, and Alexander von der Osten, were very helpful, as were Chitti Babu Buyyala, Monty Jones and Thomas Teuscher in Bouaké.

Among those who contributed to the project through interviews or in other ways were Soumaoro Bangalee, Rob Bertram, W. Ronnie Coffman, Mike Collinson, Daniel Coyne, Christopher Delgado, Alassane Diallo, Sitapha Diata, Mustapha Gaye, Robert Guei, Nils Hanssens, Jean-Yves Jamin, Dougou Keita, Simplice Kra, Joan MacNeil, Bakary Ouayogode, Thomas Randolph, Lorna Terry, Moctar Toure, Andrew Urquhart, Peter Windmeijer, and Anthony Youdeowei.

Logistical thanks are due WARDA public affairs officer Melissa Anderson for arranging transport and my schedule in Bouaké, to CGIAR librarian Danielle Lucca for cheerfully and efficiently retrieving documents and to Cimon Psira, designer, who bore with me in the preparation of the manuscript for publication. Last, unqualified thanks go to my wife, Efthalia, for her encouragement and support in this project and for everything.

Abbreviations

ADRAO	*Association pour le développement de la riziculture en Afrique de l'ouest* (French name for WARDA)
AfDB	African Development Bank
CFA	*Communauté financiére africaine* (African Financial Community)
CGIAR	Consultative Group on International Agricultural Research
CIAT	Centro Internacional de Agricultura Tropical
IRAD	*Centre de coopération internationale en recherche agronomique pour le développement*
CIMMYT	Centro Internacional de Mejoramiento de Maiz y Trigo
CORAF	*Conférence des responsables de la recherche agronomique africaine*
DANIDA	Danish Agency for International Development
FAO	Food and Agriculture Organization of the United Nations
ICRISAT	International Crop Research Institute for the Semi-Arid Tropics
IDESSA	*Institute des savanes*
IDRC	International Development Research Center
IFAD	International Fund for Agricultural Development
IFPRI	International Food Policy Research Institute
IITA	International Institute of Tropical Agriculture
ILRI	International Livestock Research Institute
INGER	International Network for the Genetic Evaluation of Rice
IRRI	International Rice Research Institute
ISRA	*Institut Sénégalais de recherches agicole*
IRAT	*Institut de recherches agronomique tropicales et des cultures vivriéres*
NERICA	NEw RIce for AfriCA
NARS	National Agricultural Research Systems
NGO	Nongovernmental Organization
RADORT	Research on Accelerated Diffusion of Rice Technology
RIDEV	Rice Development (model)
SAED	*Société national d'amenagement et d'exploitation du delta du fleuve Sénégal et des vallées du fleuve Sénégal et de la Falémé*
SRO	Sub-Regional Organization
TAC	Technical Advisory Committee of CGIAR
UNDP	United Nations Development Program
USAID	United States Agency for International Development

WARDA MEMBER COUNTRIES

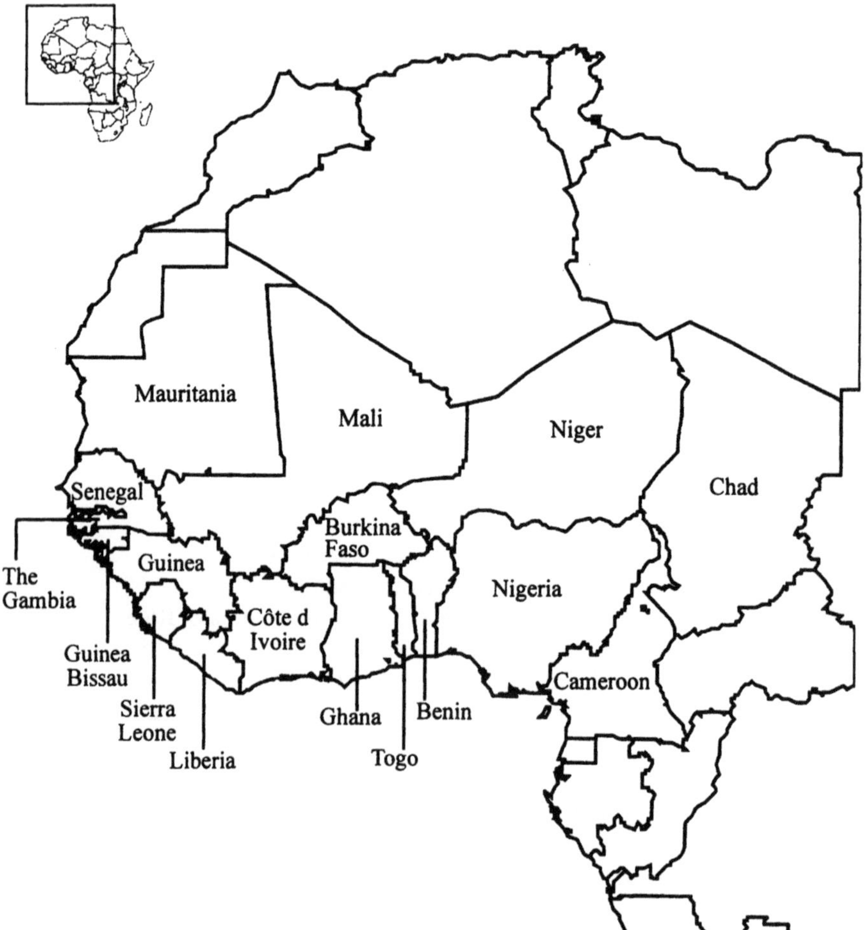

Introduction

In the spring of 1988, the West Africa Rice Development Association (WARDA) shut down its headquarters in Monrovia, Liberia and opened a temporary office in the city of Bouaké in neighboring Côte d'Ivoire as a first step in transferring operations there. The move enabled WARDA to elude the civil war that erupted two years later and brought anarchy to Liberia. It also allowed WARDA to seize a second chance, an opportunity to overcome the internal troubles that threatened its existence.

WARDA's mission, as its name suggests, is to promote agriculture in the region by helping farmers increase the production of rice. With its focus on poor farmers, WARDA contends with the Africa's central economic problem. Africa is the only continent in which population has been growing faster than food production. Much of the news out of Africa is prompted by famine, war or pestilence. But it is the shortfall in food that provokes the syndrome of poverty, hunger and violence, and the quiet crisis of the food deficit receives inadequate attention.

Many developing countries in other parts of the world have managed to increase production of food for domestic consumption sufficiently to avoid the sort of food gap that afflicts Africa. What made this possible was the so-called green revolution based on agricultural research that produced high-yielding crop varieties. The revolution was propagated by an international agricultural research system linking scientists from the industrialized countries with their counterparts in developing countries and, through them, with poor farmers there.

This international system is exemplified by the Consultative Group on International Agricultural Research. The CGIAR was established in the early 1970s on the strength of the increases in wheat and rice yields that were transforming agriculture in Asia and Latin America. WARDA is one of sixteen agricultural research centers, which now operate under the CGIAR's aegis covering the major food crops and agroecological areas of the developing world.

The CGIAR is widely regarded as an effective international development organization, but the centers made a slow start when they began operating in Africa in the 1970s. Their research strategies were ill suited to African conditions and government policies hindered the kind of innovation the international centers had to offer. The centers did recover from their early stumbles and, over the years, have adjusted to the African setting and made a number of research coups, particularly in dealing with plant diseases and pests. But Africa has still not had its green revolution.

Innovation in agriculture does not go easily in sub-Saharan Africa. The challenge is greatest in the poorest countries that have in common high rates of population growth, harsh climate, fragile soils and a lack of natural resources. A large majority of farmers follow traditional patterns, clearing a plot of land and growing crops for a few years and then moving on to allow the land to lie fallow and recover its fertility. Those practicing shifting cultivation—the more graphic term is slash and burn—typically raise enough to feed their families and a bit to barter or to sell in village markets. Improving productivity requires a leap from subsistence farming to a modernized agriculture that will produce marketable surpluses. But farmers do not own land, since it is, in effect, held communally, and, therefore, have no incentive to improve it. And they lack the resources to buy seed, fertilizer and other agricultural inputs required for intensive agriculture.

In dealing with these difficulties WARDA differed from other CGIAR centers in ways that gave it both advantages and disadvantages. Unlike the other centers that are thoroughly international entities, WARDA was founded in the early 1970s as a regional association by 11 rice-growing countries in West Africa. As a result, when WARDA finally did join the CGIAR, it was with awkward odd-man-in status.

WARDA struggled through its first decade and by 1980 was getting poor reviews for management and research and faced serious funding problems. Financially strapped West African member countries were failing to pay their dues and the donor organizations that provided the bulk of WARDA funds were increasingly reluctant to continue support without radical changes. For their part, member countries were determined to preserve WARDA's regional character. In 1986, a showdown that included some unusually candid give and take between rich and poor countries produced a compromise that granted WARDA a new, though conditional, lease on life.

To succeed, it was necessary for WARDA to build a new research center from the ground up, recruit a staff practically from scratch, and chart its course in research in a new way that would satisfy the critics. Above all, WARDA had to restore the confidence of the donors and keep the loyalty of its West African member countries.

A Harsh Climate

The times were hardly propitious for WARDA to redeem itself. Foreign aid was falling out of favor in the late 1980s and the end of the cold war eliminated superpower rivalry as the all-purpose rationale for spending on things like international agricultural research. Then a global recession struck in the early 1990s, just as WARDA was struggling to raise construction funds. Development at the M'be site near Bouaké might have stalled if WARDA's new director general, Eugene Terry, had not opted for a bolder financing strategy than was customary for the CGIAR.

If global circumstances were in an unfriendly phase, nature is a permanent peril in West Africa. In a region where climate is so harsh and soils so fragile it is hard enough to reconcile technology and ecology. But, to make its task more difficult WARDA was pledged to the new CGIAR creed of sustainability—production must be increased only in ways that do not degrade the resource base for the future.

The main challenge in human terms for WARDA and other CGIAR centers operating in Africa has been finding ways to connect with the poor farmers that the group is mandated to serve. The centers depend on national agricultural research systems, NARS, as they are styled, to relay new technologies and techniques to farmers. The weakness of the African NARS has acted as a choke point. The fault is obviously not that of the NARS alone. West African governments have failed to provide the policy framework, the transportation and market systems and the education and health services required to modernize agriculture. A lack of economic and political cooperation among countries in West Africa has also been a serious drag on development, and the divisions between former British and French territories add to the difficulties.

The ultimate aim of the CGIAR centers is to perform a successful transfer of tasks to national and regional institutions—a transaction summed up in the term devolution. The CGIAR formula has been least effective where political and economic conditions are least hospitable, and sub-Saharan Africa presents probably the roughest path to devolution. That is why WARDA's rebound after the exodus from Monrovia and nearly succumbing to problems of development endemic to the region is especially worthy of note. Despite all the impediments, WARDA not only survived but thrived. The center has earned good marks on research and management and gone a long way toward shedding its underdog image and consolidating its place in the CGIAR system. At the same time, it has retained firm support in West Africa.

How did the reborn WARDA adapt to the hard realities? First of all, WARDA's managers came to terms with the limited funding available for both program and plant. Worries that WARDA might not be able to afford the number of staff and mix of disciplines necessary to achieve critical mass made WARDA embrace innovation.

To make up for limits on staffing, WARDA styled itself an "open center." In WARDA's version, carefully selected scientists from other organizations interested in working on projects compatible with WARDA programs are invited to join WARDA and bring their own funding. WARDA also gave new substance to the currently popular concept of partnership by establishing task forces that enlist qualified researchers from national research systems and by working out a division of labor that helps both the national programs and WARDA.

Wide Crossing

Not only has WARDA been innovative organizationally, but it is making its mark squarely in the CGIAR tradition by developing improved rice varieties that will enable poor farmers in the region to increase their production of rice dramatically. The name Wide Crossing was given the WARDA rice breeding program aimed at developing a rice plant capable of both delivering high yields and doing well in the unforgiving West African growing conditions. WARDA scientists have succeeded in crossing two species of rice from widely divergent sources; such efforts have been thwarted in the past. WARDA's Wide Crossing project has been renamed NERICA (NEw RIce for AfriCA) to reflect a broad initiative aimed at promoting wide adoption of the improved rice varieties in West Africa and beyond. If, as now appears likely, expectations are borne out, what began as the Wide Crossing project will stand comparison with other major CGIAR successes in crop improvement.

In a narrow technical sense used by plant breeders, wide crossing denotes the interbreeding of two plant species. But the term also seems broadly apposite in describing WARDA itself. The center is a successful hybrid of an intergovernmental organization and a CGIAR center. It has made a crucial move from a strategy of adapting rice varieties from elsewhere to one that emphasizes developing hybrids that contain local germplasm and suit the circumstances of poor farmers in West Africa. And WARDA has reached out to combine some of its research activities with those of national programs in ways that strengthen both.

Success for a CGIAR center does not depend only on the quality of the research it performs. To accomplish its aims, a center must deal with a range of what in the vernacular of development are defined as "constraints." An important category of limiting factors falls under an environmental heading. But other constraints with which a center must contend are political, economic, social and, in West Africa, historical.

In postcolonial Africa, the past intrudes in many ways. For WARDA, the most obvious legacy is the tension generated by the privileged position of expatriate scientists and administrators. The sensitivities are in part a carryover from colonial days, but wide differences in pay and status and the slow pace of Africanization fuels the impatience of staff and officials from the region. For internationally recruited scientists, pay and perquisites are substantial, but risks go along with the benefits. Professionally, working in Africa means a detour from normal career paths at home and reentry can be difficult. Personally, problems of schooling for children and friction over spouses' careers are common. Then there is culture shock in its many manifestations and existential challenges including, in Bouaké, malaria and the occasional cobra in the garden.

These personal issues do not figure much in CGIAR policy papers or center strategy statements, but they clearly affect not only the atmospherics but the effectiveness of the centers. In WARDA's case, especially because of its split institutional personality, its handling of these matters obviously has an important impact on performance.

Lessons for the Future

At one level, WARDA can be seen as an edifying example of an institution with a troubled past and uncertain future that by pluck and luck, good ideas and hard work made a comeback against the odds. In broader perspective, WARDA may be said to have made a virtue of necessity. It not only found ways to live within its means and correct former errors, but did so in inventive ways. Although WARDA is a small and, in the larger scheme of things, obscure organization, it is a modest success story in a place where such stories are very rare. And particularly in its reinterpretation of partnership, WARDA offers some useful lessons for the future of agriculture in Africa. Above all, what WARDA's story illustrates is that the problems facing the center are not all scientific and what has determined success so far has been the ability to cope with African conditions broadly defined.

The human dimension counted heavily in WARDA's reconstruction. The new WARDA was lucky in its leaders and the choices they made. And at critical junctures it received backing from the top at the CGIAR that may well have been decisive in preserving WARDA as an independent center.

Clearly, WARDA's recovery required adherence to sound policies, but the policies pursued were not novel. What differed at WARDA was how a constellation of capable people put those ideas into action. Not to be forgotten is that those individuals, African and expatriate, were products of a system that gave them the training and experience that enabled them to make the most of the opportunities when people and circumstances came together at WARDA.

What follows is an account of WARDA's development during its second incarnation after the move to Côte d'Ivoire. It is not intended to be an institutional history in the sense of a detailed description of the evolution of WARDA's organization and program, but rather an attempt to convey how the center dealt with major challenges along the way and to tell something about the life as well as the work at WARDA.

This account is based primarily on interviews with those in both WARDA and the CGIAR who were main participants or close observers of events during the period and inevitably reflects the assessments of those individuals. The focus is mainly on the 10-year period up to the end of 1996 when the director general, Eugene Terry, and research director, Peter Matlon, whose policies and personalities had been instrumental in forming the new WARDA, were finishing their tours and a new phase was beginning. A postscript briefly describes developments at the center under its new leadership through the time of publication of the regular review of WARDA's program and management in the year 2000.

1 A Crisis Survived

From Forest to Savanna

The 350-kilometer journey by auto from Abidjan to Bouaké takes four hours more or less, depending on the daring of the driver. The road north is the national route that leads to neighboring Mali and Burkina Faso. It starts out as a showcase four-lane divided highway then becomes two-lane blacktop, well engineered and reasonably well maintained by the standards of the region. Traffic is fairly heavy, much of it trucks, buses and the vanlike bush taxis that are ubiquitous in West Africa. Many of the vehicles are old, heavily loaded and slow moving. Passing is perilous where the road twists and visibility ahead is limited. There is not much to see in the way of the works of man save for the occasional village and the town of Yamoussoukro, with the dome of its multihundredmillion-dollar basilica looking from a distance like the containment vessel of a nuclear power plant.

In the course of the trip the scenery segues from forest to savanna. Annual rainfall declines from over 1500 mm at Abidjan to around 1000 mm at Bouaké and the vegetation records the change. The forest in Côte d'Ivoire has been pillaged by a lumber industry in search of valuable hardwoods in the same way that the elephants that gave the Ivory Coast its name were virtually wiped out years ago for their tusks. In the early part of the drive, you can spot what look like tiny patches of rainforest, with vine-covered trees rising in tiers to a high canopy, suggesting what it must have once been like. Only a few remnants of true rainforest survive in Côte d'Ivoire, mostly in the southwestern corner of the country.

As you go north, the change in the landscape is so gradual as to be hardly noticeable, but past Yamoussoukro, a hundred kilometers south of Bouaké, the trees thin somewhat and the bush is less dense. Bouaké is located at the beginning of what is called the moist savanna to distinguish it from the more open scrub and grasslands of the dry savanna that begins another 400 km or so north.

From the start of the site selection committee's deliberations Côte d'Ivoire had been what WARDA director general Terry called "a high probability candidate." A major advantage was that most of the region's important rice production systems could be found within the country's borders. Côte d'Ivoire's road system is well developed by West African standards and it would, therefore, be possible to travel more easily to conduct field tests. Côte d'Ivoire's location also allows ready access to a number of WARDA's member states. It shares common borders with five of them, Burkina Faso, Ghana, Guinea, Liberia, and Mali. Electronic communications are relatively good and air transportation has been regarded as the best in the region, although the reliability of national airline schedules declined during the economic troubles of the 1980s and 1990s.

Another plus was that Côte d'Ivoire's national agricultural research system, built with French assistance, ranked as one of the best in West Africa, especially in respect to cash crops such as cotton, cocoa, coffee and rubber. A strong French research presence in the country remained. French scientists, particularly those in France's institute for research in tropical agriculture (IRAT, now CIRAD), had done substantial work on rice, and WARDA hoped to benefit from the French presence.

M'be, 35 km north of Bouaké, was picked as the site for the relocated WARDA because it is possible there to approximate the range of growing conditions with which most West African rice farmers struggle. WARDA puts a priority on helping farmers who depend on rainfall to grow rice in a range of environments—level uplands, sloping ground and swampy lowlands called inland valleys. The varied terrain and soils on WARDA's 700-hectare farm at M'be allow researchers to do field experiments across the board on what WARDA calls "the upland\inland valley continuum."

WARDA's other main research effort is on irrigated rice. Starting in the colonial era, the potential for high yields inspired ambitious and expensive irrigation projects. Most have failed abysmally. The Niger and Senegal rivers in the Sahelian countries offered inviting sources of irrigation water for such ventures in the dry zone and continue to exert an appeal. WARDA has had a team working on irrigated rice out of St. Louis in Senegal since the early 1970s, but WARDA devotes more than twice-as-much manpower and money to research on the rainfed continuum as to irrigated rice.

Climate and Geology Rule

The split between rainfed and irrigated rice territories is determined by the distribution of rainfall. West Africa lies in the monsoon belt in which dry and rainy seasons dominate the climate. The monsoon is driven by the advance and retreat of wet and dry air masses in response to seasonal changes in the relation of the earth to the sun. The rainy season in West Africa coincides roughly with the Northern Hemisphere's late spring and summer and the dry season with the autumn and winter months. In late spring, moisture drawn from the Atlantic moves northward, pushing dry air back along a line called the Inter-Tropical Convergence Zone until, in August or September, the wet air begins its retreat. Total annual rainfall decreases progressively from south to north, but yearly totals are highly variable, particularly in the north as the Sahel droughts testify.

West Africa divides into three rainfall belts running east to west. The wettest is the Guinean zone that covers large parts of the southern coastal countries and gets 1200 mm or more of rain annually, the Sudanian with total rainfall averaging between 600 and 1200 mm and the Sahelian with 400 to 600 mm or less. Growing rice under rainfed condition cannot be done safely where annual rainfall is much under 1000 mm, so rice farming in the Sahel is possible only with irrigation.

Geology as well as climate is a major factor in West African agriculture. Plains and gently rolling terrain are predominant in the landscape. The region is part of the African shield that belonged to the ancient mega-continent of Gondwanaland which split in the Mesozoic era. The section that became South America broke off from the southern coast of the present West Africa. Over the long period in which there has been little volcanic or tectonic activity in West Africa the land has been exposed to the assault of water, wind and intense heat leaving it with old soils that are infertile and degrade easily under cultivation. The great Sahel drought of the late 1960s and early 1970s drove home the natural disadvantages of West Africa and the desperate need of the newly independent countries to increase food production. This is where WARDA and the CGIAR came in.

The CGIAR and WARDA

The impetus for creating WARDA developed in the late 1960s because newly independent West African countries were spending large amounts of scarce foreign exchange to import rice, and rice consumption was rising rapidly in the fast growing and politically volatile cities. Agriculture, particularly production of food for domestic consumption, had been slighted when the novice West African governments set out to develop their economies by industrializing.

This began to change in the mid 1960s when failure of the monsoon in India and Pakistan raised the threat of famine in the subcontinent. In the years of the 1968-1972 Sahel drought, concern escalated into alarm that food production in developing countries generally was growing too slowly to keep pace with the rapid increase in population. At about the same time, the advent of high-yielding varieties of rice and wheat heralded the green revolution in Asia and Latin America, raising hopes for similar successes with other crops in other regions. This mixture of anxiety and optimism germinated the idea of the CGIAR at the end of the 1960s.

When it was created in the early 1970s, the CGIAR had to respond to the overtures of existing research organizations that wanted to join it. WARDA was one candidate. WARDA had developed separately from the CGIAR and been established at about the same time. The UN Food and Agriculture Organization (FAO) and United Nations Development Program (UNDP) had assisted 11 West African countries to form WARDA and the new organization attracted support from several of the donors that also funded the CGIAR.

In 1972, WARDA made a formal request to the CGIAR for financial assistance. WARDA, however, was an awkward applicant. It was an intergovernmental organization guided by a council of ministers of the member countries, most of them ministers of agriculture or research, not active researchers. As a regional organization it did not fit the CGIAR's international mold. Furthermore, WARDA was not a research organization in the same sense as other CGIAR centers. As the word development in its name suggests, WARDA was formed with the narrower mission of coordinating the testing and adaptation of rice varieties from elsewhere.

The CGIAR had reservations about WARDA's governance and management, but was attracted by the potential WARDA offered to connect with national research programs and by the opportunity to transfer new rice technology to West African countries. A formula under which WARDA would become part of the CGIAR was worked out and finally approved in 1976. Under it, CGIAR support would be limited to WARDA's research program, which at the time was dominated by field trials. WARDA agreed to management changes as a condition for joining, but clearly lacked the character of a CGIAR center in matters of governance and administration. In subsequent years, difficulties with funding and management kept WARDA constantly on the CGIAR agenda as a problem center and ultimately caused a full-blown institutional crisis.

WARDA In Monrovia

WARDA was in the CGIAR, but in a significant sense not of it. The center's early performance earned a mixed reaction. It had established its headquarters in Monrovia, built a training center at Fendall nearby and operated testing programs in member countries through sub-regional coordinators. WARDA introduced a number of new rice varieties that were fairly widely adopted for irrigated farming, but new varieties offered for rainfed conditions were largely ignored. Probably, WARDA's most useful venture in crop development was a mangrove rice improvement scheme at Sierra Leone's Rokupr station. The WARDA training program was regarded as the most successful of its activities.

WARDA initially lived within its means under its first executive secretary, Jacques Diouf of Senegal, who later became director general of FAO, but the 1970s proved to be a disastrous decade economically for West Africa. Drought, the increased cost of imports caused by the OPEC oil embargo and an unfavorable turn in world prices for its main exports of basic commodities hit the region hard. Governments went into debt to maintain the flow of imports, gambling that the terms of trade would turn back in their favor. They lost. Foreign debt mounted and contributions to WARDA from the region slipped into chronic arrears. By 1980, WARDA was in severe financial straits. Member countries were expected to supply about a quarter of the total budget. CGIAR funds provided about the same portion and direct support by international donors the rest. The United States Agency for International Development (USAID) in this period contributed some 30% to 40% of the total.

Alarms were slow in going off. Evaluations of WARDA in this period were done piecemeal, with donors examining only the programs they funded. Other CGIAR centers were subjected to comprehensive reviews of program and management. In the case of WARDA, the CGIAR looked only at the research it supported. These early reviewers expressed some misgivings but, by and large, gave WARDA the benefit of the doubt. Nevertheless, uneasiness was growing about both WARDA's performance and its status in the CGIAR system. When the time came for the CGIAR external review of WARDA in 1983, a decision was made to look at WARDA whole with reviews covering both scientific and management aspects of the organization.

The findings of the panel dispatched by the CGIAR's Technical Advisory Committee (TAC) to review the research program were not all adverse. The report acknowledged that WARDA had achieved some of its objectives, notably by training some 900 from the region, introducing a number of rice cultivars, establishing research programs on mangrove rice in Sierra Leone, on irrigated rice in Senegal and on rainfed rice at Bouaké and in forming viable links with national programs. The reviewers noted that WARDA was in the midst of a severe financial crisis precipitated by the failure of member countries to pay dues. Donors were also chided for picking and choosing which projects to support, thereby limiting management's ability to define and carry out a strong core program.

Lopsidedly, however, the review found fault. WARDA leadership had failed to provide an adequate operational strategy and performance criteria. Researchers were concentrated at headquarters in Monrovia and isolated from field operations. A top-heavy administration and excessive support staff leached funds from research projects. Staff morale was low, particularly at the Monrovia headquarters, where a serious division between English and French speaking staff festered.

A Strategy Found Wanting

The review made clear that in the fundamental matter of research strategy WARDA had gotten off on the wrong foot. The assumption that WARDA could act successfully as intermediary in importing and adapting rice varieties from elsewhere, notably Asia, had proved ill founded. African conditions blighted those expectations. Even when experimental rice varieties thrived in field tests on research stations, they failed in farmers' fields.

Sweeping reforms of WARDA's organization, management and scientific program were proposed. WARDA's governing council made up of officials of the member countries was declared a source of concern. Although not spelled out, the review reflected a view in the CGIAR that interference by the council in appointments and promotions had hopelessly politicized the center. The major recommendations were obviously designed to move WARDA closer to the CGIAR model. As it stood at WARDA, a scientific and technical committee that advised the governing council was made up of scientists from the member states. The review panel proposed that half the members of the committee be appointed from outside the region. The key recommendation was that the council delegate major power to the reconstituted scientific and technical committee, enabling it to function like other CGIAR boards.

In respect to research, the panel urged a drastic modification of WARDA's mandate. Instead of emphasizing the introduction and testing of exotic rice varieties, WARDA should expand its research program to include hybridization and work on identifying constraints and developing new technology for specific West African ecologies where rice could be grown. The panel also asked WARDA to formulate the integrated rice research program that had been lacking and to give priority to work on upland rice.

WARDA accepted the recommendations and promised to take immediate steps to implement them except where action by member governments was required. The CGIAR's Technical Advisory Committee endorsed the review's prescription and advised the CGIAR to continue its support of WARDA on condition that the proposed reforms be carried through on a stipulated schedule. CGIAR as a whole concurred, but it was understood within the CGIAR that WARDA was on probation and if it failed to carry out the reforms the group would likely withdraw its support.

Over the next year, WARDA made some progress on reform, but member countries continued to be delinquent in paying dues. WARDA's persisting cash flow problem cramped operations and even delayed payment of staff salaries. At the CGIAR annual centers week meeting in late 1985 donor disgruntlement was evident. The group approved WARDA's budget for only the first half of the year, clearly to put pressure on the governing council to give WARDA management greater independence of action to carry out the reforms and on member countries to meet their financial commitments. A decision on future CGIAR support for WARDA was scheduled for the CGIAR's centers week meeting a year hence.

The York Report

Inside TAC, the question of whether or not WARDA was worth supporting had been a topic of discussion for several years. Alex McCalla, who joined TAC in 1984 and went on to a 7-year tenure as chairman from 1988 to 1994, recalls that TAC members recognized that the WARDA issue was politically sensitive and required special handling. The then TAC chairman, Guy Camus, decided on an informal review that would depart from the standard TAC model for external reviews. TAC normally commissions a panel of experts who are not TAC members. In the case of WARDA, the review was to be conducted by TAC itself and chaired by TAC member E.T. York. The panel was to report to TAC, which would attach a set of comments. The review was expected to carry considerable weight when the group came to decide WARDA's fate.

Discussion of the review was on the agenda of the CGIAR's mid term meeting in Ottawa in May of 1986. Controversy over WARDA was expected, but the drama that ensued was a decided departure from the equability that normally prevails at CGIAR meetings. When the agenda reached WARDA, E.T. York led off with a summary of the review. He said that the panel had found that WARDA had taken positive actions on the reforms, but serious questions had arisen about how some of the key recommendations were being implemented. York also cited indications that the governing council had "intervened in management decisions which keeps WARDA's management from taking needed actions relating to programs and budgets." In light of these findings and WARDA's continuing financial difficulties the review panel saw little prospect of WARDA becoming an effective organization.

York said the panel recognized the need for a well integrated rice research program in West Africa and recommended that a new mechanism for meeting this need be considered, even suggesting a name, the West Africa Rice Research Institute (WARRI). The option the panel favored was creation of a new center that would combine elements of both the WARDA and the CGIAR's International Institute of Tropical Agriculture (IITA) rice research programs and have the organizational and operational characteristics of the other CGIAR centers. WARDA was to be included as one of the parties to the establishment of the new center, but, at the very least, a major loss of financial support for WARDA was clearly implied.

No TAC comment or recommendation accompanied the York report. McCalla recalls that, "In theory, the review should have gone to TAC in March and should have been presented with TAC's commentary to the group in May. But the report didn't get to TAC in time. When Mr. Camus read it he was concerned, I think that's putting it mildly, about the impact of a report that said either take WARDA away from the region and make it a freestanding center on the model of all the rest or shut it down."

A West African Response

York's presentation was followed immediately by that of the new chairman of WARDA's governing council, Ibrahima Sagna, Senegal's minister of rural development. Sagna's remarks fell somewhere between an appeal and an ultimatum. With a candor unusual in such a forum he expressed the underlying feelings of many West Africans about CGIAR conduct in the matter and about development aid in general. Sagna departed from his prepared text and the following excerpts from the official translation from the French indicate the degree to which he took exception to both the content of the report and the way it was presented. His main message was that WARDA member countries recognized the need for help from outside but resented outsiders prescribing radical change without consultation:

"I would have thought that, before these reports were to be submitted to as important an assembly as this one, they would have first of all be discussed with the established authorities of the African states, because we, in Africa, want to deal with partners on an equal footing—people who will discuss with us as responsible individuals, who will see us as people who have received the same training and the same education as they have, and who will realize that we are equally able to understand our problems and, therefore, these problems can be put on the table and discussed with us as partners rather than acting in a paternalistic fashion and saying that the Africans are not able to look after their own affairs and therefore we will have to do it for them."

Driving his point home, Sagna said "No one can create any structure in Africa without the consent of the African governments." This was his major theme, but he went on to articulate a grievance widely felt among Africans that research conducted by foreign scientists often did not benefit African countries where it was done. Declaring that "we do not want Africa to be used as a laboratory for doing research in the abstract," he went on to observe that "Pure research based simply on the desire of technological organizations to do their research without thinking of the development of the countries concerned is fine, but it really does not help us."

In concluding he combined the two themes with a warning.

"All we want is that what is done in our country should be discussed with us. Do not think we can accept a structure that would be imposed on us where people would be asked to organize certain activities within our state on the pretext of doing research adapted to the needs of African countries."

Sagna's position was that WARDA had accepted the recommendations of the external review and was moving to comply. As for the remaining requirements, these could be accommodated. Everything was negotiable except the existence of WARDA as a regional intergovernmental organization. There the West Africans drew the line.

WARDA Preserved

The CGIAR operates by consensus so it would be inaccurate to say that the Sagna speech changed votes, but it did change minds. By common assent, his statement played a crucial part in swinging sentiment behind negotiations to preserve WARDA. It had been widely understood going into the Ottawa meeting that TAC favored withdrawal of support from WARDA. No official recommendation was made and, as a consequence, the York report was never formally presented to TAC or to the group. As McCalla says, "It sort of remained in the gray literature."

For the West African countries, the decision was a victory for regional pride and a vindication of the sentiments Sagna had expressed. On the CGIAR side, the feelings were more complex and somewhat contradictory.

York, who headed the review panel, was regarded as scrupulously fair and the panel followed CGIAR canon in giving top priority to calculating how limited resources are to be used most effectively. In reprieving WARDA, the group departed from the criteria that normally governed its decision-making. CGIAR, which sees itself as an apolitical organization, clearly made a decision based on political considerations.

With the CGIAR, an element of pride was operating too. At some level the leaders of CGIAR simply did not want to see the group fail with WARDA. And hanging over the meeting was Sagna's threat of non-cooperation. As Moctar Toure representing the WARDA governing council gently phrased it at the center's meeting the next autumn, "If the break between the CGIAR and the governing council of WARDA were to occur in a crisis atmosphere, it would be very difficult for some time to mount a meaningful, independent research program in western Africa." In other words, the CGIAR could expect a cold shoulder in the region that faced the greatest need and probably posed the greatest professional challenge in respect to increasing food production.

A coincidence may have encouraged CGIAR empathy at Ottawa. The meeting took place shortly before a special session on the problems of Africa was scheduled by the UN General Assembly. Curt Farrar, who headed the CGIAR Secretariat at the time, remembers that as Sagna was making his plea "people in the hall were saying, 'can we go to the General Assembly two weeks from now and say we've just sunk WARDA and its 16 member countries?'"

Over the next six months the essentials of a compromise were thrashed out. World Bank vice-president David Hopper, who had taken over as CGIAR chairman, sought help with the task from Canada's International Development Research Centre. Through the IDRC's good offices, Moise Mensah of Benin was asked to use his diplomatic skills and knowledge of the region to canvass WARDA member countries on the possibilities for reaching agreement. Mensah proved a successful intermediary and Farrar and Camus shuttled frequently to West Africa to fashion a formula acceptable to all parties.

Under the agreement, which was endorsed by the group at its meeting in Washington in late 1986, WARDA remained a regional, intergovernmental organization. The council of ministers retained ultimate authority over WARDA, but management of the center and its research program was recast on the model of the other CGIAR centers, very much as the 1983 external review had recommended. Broad authority was shifted from the governing council to a board of trustees evolved from the scientific and technical committee and internationalized by appointment of half its members from outside the region. It was understood that the reorganized board and CGIAR would jointly oversee the formulation of a new research strategy for WARDA.

A sticking point in the negotiations had been the criteria for appointing the WARDA director general, an issue with heavy symbolic overtones. West African countries insisted that only West Africans be eligible for the post while the CGIAR strongly preferred that the DG be recruited internationally, as was the case for other centers. The compromise agreed upon was that the director general be a citizen of a WARDA member country but not necessarily a resident.

At Ottawa, WARDA had won the day, but received a less than overwhelming vote of confidence. It was clear that there were many hurdles in the path ahead for the new WARDA and there were still skeptics in the CGIAR and among the donors who doubted that WARDA would survive in the longer run and who would be watching closely and in perhaps a not too friendly way.

Toward a New WARDA

The first order of business for the new WARDA was the selection of a board and a director general. The new board, divided evenly between West African and international members, apparently meshed well. Moctar Toure, who headed Senegal's agricultural research institute, was the first chairman of the reconstituted board. He is credited with being responsive both to regional sensitivities and to the concern of international members that WARDA achieve high standards in research. In his year as chairman, Toure presided over the key appointments of director general and director of research. The choice for director general was Eugene Robert Terry, a Sierra Leonean then 49. Trained as a plant pathologist, Terry at the time was director of international cooperation and training at the CGIAR's International Institute of Tropical Agriculture (IITA) at Ibadan in Nigeria.

Terry says that his first inkling of the WARDA job came in March of 1986 from none other than E.T. York, who was representing TAC at an IITA board meeting. York and his panel had completed their report on WARDA, but the definitive Ottawa meeting was still two months ahead. "I did not even know that there had been a mid-term review of WARDA," says Terry. York took Terry aside and told him that the panel had recommended that WARDA be replaced by a new center. He then went on to say to Terry, "I've proposed a profile of the person who should head it and I think you fit that. Would you be interested in accepting the nomination if I am asked to nominate somebody?"

Terry responded by saying, "I wasn't expecting this kind of a question so let me ponder it. I went home and talked to my wife and told her that what I'd heard of WARDA recently was that it was on its last legs and was going to be suppressed." Terry's remark reflected what was probably a consensus in the CGIAR at the time. He said he was inclined to tell York that he was not interested. "We talked about it that evening and my wife said to me, 'That's a rather quick decision you've made. Why don't you find out a few more things from E.T.'"

Terry had a further conversation with York and asked about the chances for moral and financial support from the CGIAR and donor community. York replied that he thought they were good. With that assurance, Terry gave a tentative yes to being nominated and it was left at that. "I did not go to the Ottawa meeting so I did not know all of that drama that took place." The next thing Terry heard was "that they had decided that they would go with WARDA, they would not suppress it."

After the agreement was concluded between the WARDA member countries and CGIAR, the job description for the director general's post was defined. Terry says he overcame his reluctance to leave a secure and interesting job at IITA and formally applied. Interviews for the post were held in Monrovia in March 1987 at the end of WARDA's annual rice review that brought together rice scientists from WARDA and from other programs in the region. During the meeting, a rumor circulated that the job would go to one of the other finalists. The suspense soon ended, however, when a member of WARDA's board arrived at IITA to tell Terry he had been selected.

The appointment still had to be approved by WARDA's governing council. It would be the first time that the board selected and the council appointed WARDA's head and there was some uneasiness. All went smoothly. The council gave its approval at a meeting in June of 1987 and Terry moved to Monrovia that September.

Relocation Resisted

When he joined WARDA Terry had to prepare immediately for a meeting of the council of ministers that month in Dakar to talk about a new location for WARDA. "I had been briefed by the board that one of the things in the cards was to look for a site to develop the new WARDA because downtown Monrovia was not the most appropriate site for the West African rice research organization."

Relocation, however, entailed decamping from Monrovia and WARDA was immediately plunged into, arguably, the touchiest site selection process that any CGIAR center has gone through. A site selection committee appointed by the board came to the Dakar meeting prepared to report to the council.

"They duly made their recommendation based on their review of scientific evidence, rainfall, soil types, logistic parameters. They said M'be near Bouaké in Côte d'Ivoire is the best site to locate the main research center and headquarters of WARDA," says Terry. "Liberia protested strenuously. The Liberian minister said the scientific and technical reasons given for the recommendation were not valid, that it was political, that Côte d'Ivoire was lusting after WARDA for the longest while, anyway, and this was just their latest move to steal the organization away from Liberia."

Reacting to this objection, the council decided that WARDA management should commission an independent review team to look at the site selection committee's recommendation. This was not to be a detailed reevaluation of the sites but rather a "desk review" of the recommendations to be conducted in Monrovia. The review panel was chaired by WARDA board member W. Ronnie Coffman of Cornell University and included a geologist who was a Liberian.

This set up what Terry calls "a memorable meeting" of the council in December of 1987. The meeting was held in Lagos because a Nigerian soldier, Brigadier Dado Nasco, was scheduled to take over as council chairman from Sagna. Coffman was brought in to present the findings of his panel. He reported that the review panel had unanimously endorsed the site selection committee's recommendations. Again, the Liberian minister protested and, as the council moved to approve a resolution accepting the committee's recommendation, he appeared to be moving toward a physical confrontation with the chairman. At this point, Sagna turned the gavel over to the new chairman. The Liberian minister then argued that such a major decision as relocation should be made by heads of state not by the council. When he was told that the council had been given the mandate to make such decisions he walked out of the meeting. At that, the resolution designating the Bouaké area for the new site was approved.

After the acrimonious meeting in Lagos, the task of transferring WARDA's headquarters and most of its operations to Côte d'Ivoire looked anything but easy. Terry says that before the Lagos meeting, Liberian officials told him that if the decision went against Liberia "the Liberian government and people will not be able to take responsibility for the safety of WARDA and its personnel." CGIAR leaders were concerned that Terry in particular might be targeted.

Tensions in Monrovia

The departure of WARDA was an especially sensitive issue at the time.

The Liberian government headed by Master Sergeant Samuel Doe was experiencing the difficulties that led to the outbreak of civil war in 1989 and the killing of Doe and a number of government officials. Terry says that he took two main security measures. In Monrovia, WARDA shared a building in a compound with the United Nations Development Program. "I told UNDP that as they were one of the cosponsors of WARDA I'm going to put our safety and wellbeing in their hands. And they accepted. The other thing I did was to move my family to Sierra Leone for that Christmas period. It was Christmas anyway, so it was a good excuse. My family was just going home for Christmas. But that was a security move also."

Terry returned to Monrovia at the beginning of 1988 without incident. He then went to Nigeria to meet with the new council chairman to discuss how to break the news officially of the relocation to President Doe and also to get a letter from the council chairman formally asking Côte d'Ivoire to give permission for WARDA to start the process of establishing itself there.

In the negotiations with Doe, a gambit that proved crucial was a letter signed by Nigeria's head of state, General Ibrahima Babangida, informing Doe of the council's decision and asking him not to stand in the way. And other ways were sought to cushion the blow. "In fact, there were going to be three things left to show we were not jumping ship and abandoning Liberia altogether," says Terry. These were the training center in Fendall built by USAID, a small germplasm unit attached to the center and a significant WARDA presence in Liberia's central agricultural research institute at Suakoko.

Terry says that the letter from Babangida was the main factor in softening up Doe. "When we eventually did go with the minister from Nigeria and the letter was presented it was very dramatic. Doe sits on a chair up high and we all sit low down looking up at him. He read the letter and put it down and said, 'Hmmm, this is from my brother, my big brother Babangida. He's explaining to me that this is all technical and scientific reasons why WARDA has to move. Nothing to do with politics. We had been told it was a political thing. The French and Côte d'Ivoire wanted to take this away from Liberia for political reasons, but it is all technical. And I never want to be accused of standing in the way of technical progress. So I will send you back, Mr. chairman of council, to tell my brother Babangida that I accept and I will do all possible to make this move possible.'

"But then he turned to me and said, 'But you, Mr. Director General, you are the one who is a book man so you have to go and explain to the Liberian people why you are moving. After all the Liberian people are not happy. After 17 years of supporting you they will wonder why you are moving. So you have to explain to them.'

"And I said, I accept, sir. I will do that. So that was it. And true to his word, all the papers that needed to be signed for us to move without harm or hindrance he signed. And the last major thing that happened in Liberia was the press conference arranged by the minister of agriculture." As it turned out, it was the minister, not Terry, who dealt with the press. Terry had suggested that if he spoke it would appear that he was simply trying to justify the move and it would be better if the minister were the spokesman.

Terry says that he briefed him thoroughly and the minister did "a wonderful job." This was the same person who nearly started a brawl with Sagna in Lagos. But Terry observes that the minister had, understandably, been playing a role. Doe's situation at the time was desperate. "A lot of organizations were moving out of Liberia. USAID was folding up. He was in real trouble. And with WARDA, a regional organization, he couldn't say it's just these white people who don't like to see a black man in power." In early May, Terry says, "We packed up lock, stock and barrel and moved out of Liberia. We hired trucks and packed files, filing cabinets, tables, chairs. We didn't attempt to be very selective. We just packed everything before they changed their minds."

Starting Over in Côte d'Ivoire

Meanwhile, permission had been sought in Côte d'Ivoire to open negotiations on a location for WARDA. Some ambiguity in the government's position had emerged earlier when the Liberians accused Côte d'Ivoire of trying to steal WARDA from them. Ivorian President Felix Houphouet-Boigny had made a somewhat delphic statement that his country was not seeking to be host to WARDA. When Terry traveled to Abidjan to open discussions, it became apparent that the president had been doing the diplomatically tactful thing and distancing himself from controversy. During Terry's first session in the ministry of agriculture and animal resources, which was designated to oversee discussions with WARDA, telephone contact was made with the president. Terry says the president was informed that the WARDA council was officially requesting that WARDA be established in Côte d'Ivoire. "The president replied that in that case he would not stand in the way and said please facilitate the move."

Besides dealing with a change of venue for WARDA, an early challenge for the new director general was to take the lead in formulating a 10-year research strategy for the center. Ever since the 1983 external review, WARDA had been encouraged to pay much more attention to upland rice, that is rice grown by poor farmers under rainfed conditions usually in combination with other crops. The reflexive CGIAR tendency was to favor cropping systems that promised maximum yields. This typically required water control and ample use of agricultural chemicals. The old WARDA had accordingly put emphasis on irrigated rice and mangrove or swamp rice.

Terry says that when work on a new strategy began it was clear that upland rice presented the toughest challenge, "but 60 percent or more of the people who produce rice in West Africa were producing it in upland systems." Upland rice is not grown under a single regime. The gently rolling landscape of West Africa often means that a rice farmer may have to contend with varied growing conditions created by differences in grade, soil and water conditions on the land he is cultivating.

The Continuum Concept

"We decided to look on this as a continuum of production systems." says Terry. "The continuum concept is based on a toposequence or land forms." Three sorts of terrain make up the continuum. Uplands, where rice is grown under rainfed conditions on fairly level ground where the water table never rises to the root zone. Hydromorphic conditions, land on a grade where the water table fluctuates but rice plants are never submerged. And lowland areas, also known as inland valleys, where rice plants are submerged for a major part of the growing season. "At any given time a farmer can be producing rice in any one of those three ecosystems or in all three. Often, he grows other crops in association with rice. In fact, that is why our mandate is to develop technology for rice production systems, not just for the rice crop."

There was solid grounding for the strategy. W. Ronnie Coffman, a charter member of the new WARDA board and chairman of its program committee, had earlier done a review of rice research in West Africa for TAC and the WARDA board that focused on upland rice and, in effect, staked out the lines for a new strategy. Coffman, a rice breeder who worked at IRRI, went on to Cornell to become director of research in the College of Agriculture there. Alex McCalla, who was a member of TAC at the time, recalls that Coffman "had taken a very hard look at what the science issues in upland rice were in West Africa and what potential there was for a scientific contribution.

"Basically, he argued that the traditional IRRI model, which was to increase the capacity of the plant to absorb fertilizer and, thereby, increase yield, wasn't going to work there. You would have to have more of a systems approach, give a lot of attention to soil and drainage and agronomic crop improvement programs rather than just genetics or breeding-based crop improvement.

"He said what you really ought to be focusing on is the potential for rice production in favored areas in the region. The favored areas he saw were these so-called inland valleys and hydromorphic areas, of which there are a lot in West Africa in the border between the savanna and the humid areas."

The new WARDA strategy "evolved collectively out of the program committee interacting with Gene Terry and with Peter Matlon (WARDA's director of research), in particular," said Coffman. "Another person who was influential was Louise Fresco." Also a board member, Fresco, an agronomist from Wageningen Agricultural University in the Netherlands, went on to become director of the research, extension and training division at FAO. Coffman says, "We came to agreement that breeding, which had been the cornerstone of IRRI's achievements in Asia, was not going to be the sole solution in West Africa. We had to look at resource management and the continuum. Louise, is an agronomist with a lot of experience in West Africa. I would credit her with holding our feet to the fire that resource management was equally important to breeding and you were not going to get major achievements out of breeding unless you paid attention to resource management."

Matlon recalls the contribution made by a mission sent by the CGAIR that included Klaus Lampe, who later became director general of IITA, and Hubert Zandstra, who went on to become DG of the International Potato Center (CIP). Matlon says WARDA owes a debt to the mission report that, he says, "provided the fundamentals we're still working on." Coffman notes that there was plenty in the rice research literature pointing to the continuum, the direction that WARDA decided to go. But nobody had succeeded in mastering the difficulties it presented. WARDA, of course, also conducts research on irrigated rice, but it is its work on the continuum that will determine WARDA's ultimate success or failure.

Eugene Terry

Eugene Terry's ascent to the director generalship of WARDA is worth noting not so much as a personal success story but as an illustration of how an international system that developed after World War II enabled him to gain the education and experience that prepared him for the challenges at WARDA. Early on, by his own ability and the timely assistance of others he made the most of the limited opportunities available and was well placed when the horizon of opportunity widened in the 1960s.

Terry is a member of the first generation of Africans with advanced degrees to make careers in agricultural research. Even after World War II, higher education institutions in Africa did not offer graduate work in agricultural sciences. The few Africans who studied abroad prepared for careers in law, medicine or business. After the independence watershed years of the early 1960s, agricultural research institutions in West Africa continued to depend on expatriate scientists. It was only as food production lagged that educational opportunities in the field increased. In part, this came about because one form that cold war competition took in Africa was the offer of training abroad.

Born in Sierra Leone in 1937, Terry came of age in the twilight years of colonial rule. He was not a member of an ethnic group as are most West Africans who identify themselves as Hausa, Yoruba, Wolof, Manding, Bambara, etc. Terry is descended from people brought to Sierra Leone by the British who had established a settlement there for freed slaves in the early 19th century. Some were taken from slave ships on the high seas by British navy anti-slavery patrols. Others had been held in slavery in the Caribbean or England and then emancipated and returned to "the colony," as it was known. One of the characteristics of this latter group, says Terry, "is that they have slave names. Jones, Johnson, Terry, Coker, McCloud, for example. Some of them had acquired an education in England, so the British used them as managers." These families achieved prominence in the society that many members of the group maintained. British influence remained strong when Terry was a boy. He grew up and went to school in Freetown, where he attended the leading secondary school, the Church Missionary Society Grammar School. After graduation in 1955, he worked for a year in the government railway department and then went to England.

In London, Terry says he was looked after by an uncle who was working on a doctorate in chemistry and an aunt who was a hospital administrator. Aiming to qualify for university entrance, Terry enrolled at the polytechnic that in later years became the University of Elephant and Castle on London's South Bank. He says that he "worked by day and went to school at night. I was a lab technician, working in a food chemistry lab to start with and then in plastics chemistry."

He cleared the hurdles of the O-level and A-level exams required for university entrance and was accepted by Nottingham University. However, when Terry applied for a Sierra Leone government scholarship he was told that, since he had managed well so far and had family help, the few available scholarships would go to those with greater need. Fortunately for the disappointed Terry, an education attaché at the embassy was sympathetic and suggested an alternative. Commonwealth countries had begun to offer competitive scholarships to students from present and former colonial possessions.

The most lucrative scholarships were offered by Canada and the attaché said he would submit Terry's papers to the Canadian universities. This was the first in a series of interventions by people in positions of authority who clearly saw promise in Terry and which had crucial impact on his career.

To the New World

With A-levels in chemistry, physics and zoology and acceptance at Nottingham to read for a degree in agriculture, Terry was a strong candidate. Word came back that he had won a scholarship. "And so I chose McGill," says Terry. "I didn't know very much about it, but I liked the fact that it was an English-speaking university in a French-speaking province." He arrived in Quebec in September of 1961. Because of his A-levels he was granted exemption from freshman year and was able to complete his degree in three years instead of four. He majored in plant pathology. Toward the end of his last year Terry got a letter from the Sierra Leone embassy noting that he was due to graduate and regulations required that, on completion of a first degree, he return to Sierra Leone to serve his country.

Terry went to the dean, George Dionne, who told him that he thought Terry should go to graduate school. As he put it, with few like Terry coming across, they should exploit the potential. The dean offered to write to the powers in Ottawa and the Sierra Leone embassy in Washington. The answer from Ottawa was that they were reluctant not to follow the rules, but since it was the dean who made the request and not the student they were willing to make an exception if the Sierra Leone embassy agreed.

The response from Sierra Leone was long in coming. While he waited that summer, Terry worked cutting grass, cleaning houses and whatever came to hand. Finally, the exception was granted in a decision apparently made by the minister of education and Terry started work on a master's degree in nematology. In 1966, he finished his thesis, got married, and left Canada all in the same week. He had met his wife, Lorna, a native of St. Vincent in the West Indies, in Montreal. After exactly 10 years away he headed home to Sierra Leone and the teaching job he had been awarded on condition that his master's degree was granted.

Terry says he enjoyed his time at McGill. The faculty of agriculture is not on the main campus in Montreal but in a town some 20 km west of the center of the city. Enrollment was small, some 1500, and included students in home economics and education. "Montreal had almost all the things you would want in a big metropolis," says Terry, without the atmosphere of a New York or

Chicago. He concedes he found the climate trying. Having spent time in England, "I was used to winter but not the kind of winters in Canada. So I did suffer, yes. I hibernated quite a bit in the winter."

The return to Sierra Leone took some adjusting. N'jala University College, where Terry was to teach, is 126 miles from Freetown. "I was a real city boy, I hadn't traveled much in the country. But I loved it, took to it, it was a peaceful life. I caught malaria, yes. I'd been away from malaria for so long, you get knocked down by that and by a few other things that the system was not adapted to." Word that he had won his master's degree soon came through and after a year on the job he was told that he would be going to the University of Illinois to do a doctorate. Terry had been picked in one of the institution building programs that were in fashion then, this one sponsored by the U.S. Agency for International Development (USAID). Illinois was paired with N'jala and, as Terry puts it, "I was part of the human resources development program."

Terry arrived at Illinois in 1967 and received his doctorate in 1970. Champaign-Urbana in those years was not as tranquil a place as McGill had been. Terry was elected president of the African student association and, because it was the time of the Biafra war in Nigeria, he wryly recalls it as "my first leadership position. It was my job to keep the various Nigerian factions apart. The politics and the bitterness came down to that level of student life even in foreign universities."

Another part of the president's job was to bring the university's black student association and the African student association together, Terry says. "We started to find what things we had in common, and how we could profit from each other." Terry and his organization were involved in one of the original affirmative action programs. As a result of the Koerner commission study on race relations, says Terry, "the University of Illinois had dedicated themselves to pick up 500 black students and give them immediate coaching. We were one of the groups—the Africans—picked to help teach these kids in math and science. Up to then, all the black kids knew about Africa was what they had seen in Tarzan movies. So that was a good experience."

Terry remembers vividly the impact the events of those years had on the university. "I was there when Martin Luther King was killed. I was there when Robert Kennedy was killed and when the Kent State incident happened. All the universities seemed to rise up with one mind and protest against the Vietnam war. After the killings at Kent State there was wholesale rioting, violent protests. A curfew was declared and the National Guard sent in to maintain order." Terry says that not everything was negative. "Some healing started. A lot more blacks talked to a lot more whites. There were joint meetings. The Africans got involved, shared some of the concerns of the blacks and we got closer together." But as for the coaching program, he says regretfully that of the 500, he "eventually heard that only 25 percent of them stayed."

New Horizons

When Terry completed his doctorate he returned to Sierra Leone and the same job. The university had recommended him for the scholarship and released him to go and he had signed a bond to come back for three years. Hardly had he returned when he was asked to attend a meeting of young nematologists at IITA in Nigeria. Terry's doctoral work had been in the transmission of virus diseases in plants, but he had been invited to the meeting because he had done his masters in nematology.

Soon after, he got a letter from the director general of IITA saying that Terry might not have realized it but the DG was conducting a job interview when he had spoken to Terry at the nematology meeting. Positions for plant pathologists were open at IITA and Terry was encouraged to apply. Terry wrote back saying it would have been an honor to come and work at IITA, but he was committed to the government of Sierra Leone for three years. He indicated, however, that he would be open to an offer at the end of that time. Three years later IITA did resume the discussion, saying that there were positions open and he might like to apply. Terry did, was interviewed for two positions and opted for the post of pathologist in the root crops program.

At IITA he went to work with a well-known Korean researcher, Dr. Sang Ki Hahn from Seoul University, to develop plant pathology programs for cassava, yam and sweet potatoes. Their larger aim was to create a root crop program for Africa that would eventually involve a network of scientists from all the national programs in countries in which root crops were staple foods. Terry was responsible for recruiting scientists from national programs for joint activities so that they could benefit from the new technology coming out of IITA.

When the root crops network was solidly established, Terry was picked to head IITA's outreach program designed to link up national programs for technology diffusion. Terry says, "I soon found out that scientists were not the best collaborators. They were invariably so busy with their research that the cooperation part of it was left either to chance or was done very badly, top down." The insights he gained on the need for structure were to influence the shape of the partnership programs developed when he moved to WARDA.

In 1981, Terry became IITA's director of international cooperation with the task of developing a cohesive international cooperation program with national scientists at the center of the program. Training was added to his responsibilities so that he was director of international cooperation and training when he left to take over at WARDA.

WARDA guest house was used as headquarters when the center first moved to Bouaké in 1988. It now accommodates trainees and visitors to the center.

Sign at entrance of guest house indicates WARDA\ADRAO's bilingual mandate. Guest house is located in Kennedy quarter of Bouaké on the outskirts of the city.

Soon after move to Côte d´Ivoire WARDA director general Eugene Terry (right) and board members survey land at M´be where WARDA farm will be established.

UN Food and Agriculture Organization director general Jacques Diouf (pointing) on visit to WARDA. Diouf was WARDA's first executive secretary in Monrovia.

2 Building a New WARDA

A Task With Many Dimensions

At the new WARDA, formative decisions on refining a strategy, recruiting a staff and constructing facilities all had to be taken at more or less the same time. With WARDA under close scrutiny, it was crucial that the right people be picked for the tasks at hand. As for strategy, the intention from the start was that operations of the new WARDA be better attuned to West African conditions. WARDA would not rely on improving crops simply through traditional plant breeding methods, but would adopt a much more comprehensive approach, taking into account environmental factors such as climate, soil, and water. Greater attention would also be given to economic and political conditions in the region and much closer collaboration with institutions and individual researchers in member countries was to be sought. Scientists and support staff had to be able to meet the requirements of a changed research agenda and it soon became clear that there would be no place at the new WARDA for many of the old hands.

After consulting with the board, Terry moved promptly to fill two key positions, director of research and director of finance. Both of the persons chosen had experience in West Africa and Terry knew both. The new director of finance was Gordon MacNeil, a Canadian who was then working as a program officer for Canada's International Development Research Center (IDRC). As Terry puts it, "We were looking for a five-legged sheep. We wanted somebody who could be at home in administration as well as finance. Gordon was more an administration man, but he quickly picked up financial management." MacNeil set up new administrative and financial systems, which had been weak points of the old WARDA. The panel that conducted the external review of WARDA in 1993 lauded the result. Terry says of MacNeil that "to his credit, as a result of the fine job he did at WARDA the CGIAR Secretariat pinched him." MacNeil joined the Secretariat as a financial officer in Washington 1993 and moved to IRRI in 1998.

Terry's choice for research director was Peter J. Matlon an American with a doctorate in agricultural economics and substantial experience in West Africa with CGIAR's International Crops Research Institute for the

Semi-Arid Tropics (ICRISAT). Matlon, who was 42 when he joined WARDA, had served from 1979 to 1986 as principal economist and West African economics program leader based at ICRISAT's outstation near Ouagadougou in Burkina Faso. At WARDA, Matlon was given responsibility for coordinating the recruiting effort and formulation of the medium term plan covering five years (1990-1994). He and Terry defined the disciplines needed based on the priorities laid out in the plan.

A Winnowing Process

The most highly charged issue was that of staffing. WARDA's board made some reductions in staff in Monrovia, but virtually all the remaining international staff moved to Bouaké, says Terry. "They all came knowing very well that I was going to declare all of their positions open. It was made clear from the beginning that those positions were going to be subject to international recruitment. That was a very important step. It was a board decision and I had to implement it. It was tense."

Although the WARDA staff members who made the transfer to Bouaké knew that all positions would be open, they hoped that their service through hard times would count in their favor. Terry recalls that their attitude was "'You know we have to be given special consideration because we stuck with this organization during the worst times and some of us went without salary for five months and we continued working.' I had to say, Sorry, the job is going to be declared open. You are welcome to apply."

A dilemma for the new management was that, though determined to give no guarantees to incumbents, a mass exodus would stall the work of the center. Some programs were productive and the aim was to capitalize on them to show that WARDA was a viable organization even as recruiting went forward. Most staff members were willing to soldier on.

As the winnowing process began, it was clear that the specialties of a number of staff scientists would not fit WARDA's new strategy. Also, Matlon says, a discouraging pattern emerged when he looked at staff members' publications records and what they had otherwise done professionally. Most had earned doctorates from excellent universities and produced a number of internationally refereed publications soon after receiving their Ph.D.s. "Then, zip," says Matlon. "Their scientific output slid dramatically after several years at WARDA. They appeared to have lacked strong scientific guidance and quality control. I felt badly for people who had obviously been highly competitive earlier. But many of them, once well into their careers, had lost their scientific edge, not all of them, but a majority."

So that the old WARDA scientific staff would feel they had been given a fair chance to compete, Terry and Matlon declared that all who reapplied for positions would be short-listed and go through an interview. Only two were retained. One of whom, Kouame Miezan, then a rice breeder in the upland rice program at Bouaké, heads WARDA's Sahel program.

Departures and Arrivals

As the bad news was delivered, there were the inevitable painful moments. Terry remembers "Some people were, of course, antagonistic at times to me and to my wife. 'Now that we are about to see the Promised Land you are kicking us out.' I could only explain to them that I was following board policy. We went on with the recruitment. Bit by bit, one by one. It wasn't done en masse so it didn't look too dramatic. You could see old faces leaving with the usual sendoff. Sometimes with tight lips and not very pleasant faces, but we had to do it. And new faces started to come."

A recruiting shopping list was based on WARDA's new medium-term plan which specified the number of positions, the disciplines and tasks. Matlon says, "We developed profiles at that time for 17 positions and started advertising in late '89 for the positions that were to be recruited in 1990. The plan called for bringing in two or three additional people a year until we reached our full complement in, I think, year four of the plan." That projection proved wildly optimistic.

The response had been gratifying. "For the 17 positions advertised we received 1100 applicants," says Matlon. "We were very pleased, I think it was a reflection of confidence, because we had a lot of good applicants. The applications were assessed with the help of outside experts in various disciplines and five or six candidates were short listed for each position. Terry and Matlon then went on the road to conduct interviews in each major region of the world. Matlon says, "It was tiring, but it was also exciting to see the quality of scientists who wanted to take a chance on the new WARDA."

An Interdisciplinary Bias

WARDA's sights were set high. Matlon says that they were looking for "world class people" who would be hired readily by any international research institute. "So we were looking for people who had exceptionally strong educational backgrounds, references, publications, who had proved that they could deliver."

Also looked for were "people who appreciated and wanted to work in an interdisciplinary environment, who didn't have disciplinary blinders on. In the interviews we did as much as we could to explore that side of it until we could get beyond what they thought the interviewers wanted to hear. We were also looking for people who were committed to working with national programs, who had a sense of being a teacher and who were instinctive collaborators. We tried to tease that out in the interviews.

"Finally, I wanted to get 75 or 80 percent of the staff who were quite young, maybe within two or three years of getting their Ph.D.s, for several reasons. One, I wanted them to be state of the art in terms of their training. Two, I wanted them to have a lot of energy so that they could do field work and not feel it a sacrifice to get out into the villages, but actually have a curiosity that comes with youth and want to be out there. Three, I wanted people who, being young, had to produce. That first 10 years after your Ph.D. you have got to produce a number of significant publications. You've got to demonstrate what you can do. If you hired too many people who are well established, they could coast. I wanted people who were hungry."

As leavening, he says that WARDA also sought "a couple of people who were well known in the world in terms of having delivered, senior rice scientists who could provide guidance to the younger people and some early credibility to WARDA. When you look at who we brought in they generally fit this profile."

Limits on Tenure

Researchers competing for positions at WARDA do so in the knowledge that there are fixed time limits on appointments. Open-ended employment had resulted in the accumulation of deadwood at some CGIAR centers and trimming was difficult. With board backing, WARDA management implemented a policy intended to signal that scientists were expected to continue to be professionally productive. The rationale was that recruiting people who were disposed to meet that challenge and then move on was a good formula for achieving WARDA's goals. The policy applies only to internationally recruited staff.

New hires are offered a contract for two years, which, in effect, is a probationary period. If their performance is satisfactory, their contracts are extended for an additional three years. At the end of that time, a very thorough evaluation of their work is made. A positive assessment means that a terminal contract for up to six years can be offered. So a researcher's maximum time at WARDA is 11 years. Matlon says he thinks that WARDA was among the first of the international centers to adopt such a policy. Limits on tenure are a subject of controversy in the CGIAR, but some other centers have adopted provisions similar to WARDA's.

When the time for actual hiring came, WARDA's budget squeeze made it possible to recruit only nine of the projected 17 scientific staff members. All but two first choices accepted. In one of those cases, that of a woman who was deemed the strongest candidate for the position in question, the issue was the contemporary quandary of a lack of a job for her spouse. She took a post at another CGIAR center where her husband was also offered an appointment.

Despite a CGIAR program to encourage the recruiting of women, the CGIAR centers generally have had limited success in hiring women in agricultural science specialties. This is attributed in part to competition for the relatively small number of women in the field. Also, women may find work at a center a poor fit with their individual or family circumstances. In another case at WARDA, where a woman was the top-rated candidate and was offered a scientist's post, she declined mainly on the grounds that she was single and social opportunities in Bouaké were too restricted. The CGIAR record is somewhat better in respect to the hiring of women social scientists. WARDA in 1997 had two women economists on its staff, one a Rockefeller postdoctoral fellow on the WARDA Sahel team, the other at M'be on a shared appointment with her husband.

After the initial rounds of hiring, the general feeling at WARDA was that, on balance, the recruits met the high standards that had been set. Of the original appointments to the new WARDA staff, equal proportions were African, Asian, and European\North American. "A good rainbow coalition," Matlon observes. One of the original hires was terminated after two years. This scientist had an excellent record in working with farmers and with national programs, but his interests did not jibe with the WARDA program in which he worked. Matlon admits to some relief at the time that the person happened to be an American since it might well have been more awkward for him if someone who was not a compatriot had been terminated. "It was difficult because he and his family became very well established when the community was only about nine scientists. They were very outgoing, very social. It induced some shock waves socially when they left. But I think that an important point was made."

Apprehension about one aspect of this first round of hiring on the international circuit proved misplaced. Matlon says that WARDA was put under absolutely no pressure by WARDA member countries to hire on anything other than a competitive basis, although this proved not to be altogether true of the donors. The absence of regional interference in center affairs at this crucial point added to confidence that, indeed, it was a new day for WARDA.

Land Dispute at M'be

The Bouaké area had early been designated as the preferred place for WARDA's headquarters and main experiment station, but a specific location had not been settled on. The old WARDA's upland rice program had operated for a decade at Côte d'Ivoire's Institute de Savanes (IDESSA) station west of Bouaké. The land there was not suitable for larger scale development and government officials had identified land at M'be 35 km north of Bouaké that appeared to meet WARDA's requirements admirably. Although the area was not densely populated, the predictable dispute over land rights erupted and tortuous three-way negotiations began involving WARDA, the government and local villagers.

The government had indicated a 3000-hectare area within which land would be provided and told WARDA management in 1989 that it could immediately choose 100 hectares inside the larger area to begin development. How much additional land WARDA would get became the subject of an extended haggle. WARDA managers who were involved in the negotiations tend to be pained but restrained when asked about the dynamics. Four villages lay within a two-to-three km radius of the projected WARDA farm. Three of the four villages immediately welcomed WARDA's arrival. One village, Konankro, did not. It stood to lose over 300 ha, perhaps 60 or 70 ha of which were being cultivated.

The dispute had several dimensions. Some villagers appeared to feel that WARDA was a wealthy organization that was paying people off at different levels and they simply wanted a share. The village was also split between the elders and the young. By and large, the young people wanted WARDA there. The elders did not. Among the cultural reasons for opposition was that, as the elders said, they were yam people, not rice people. The idea of losing good yam land to those working in rice struck them as blasphemous. The major underlying issue was that, although the villagers were actively cultivating only a small fraction of the available land at any time, they were determined to preserve access for their descendants.

M'be is in slash-and-burn farming territory and local villagers cultivated fields on the site but did not live there. Land tenure in the area follows the general West African pattern under which ownership has a duality confusing to outsiders. Traditionally, ownership of land resides with a group or extended family; rights to crops on a particular piece of land belong to those who cultivate it.

Independence brought a further complication. Governments asserted authority over all land, at least all rural land. In practice, traditional land tenure customs are still widely observed, so resolving conflicts like that over a transfer of land to WARDA often requires long negotiation. WARDA is not alone in being involved in land disputes. Other CGIAR centers have been caught in longer running and more acrimonious ones.

Reaching an Accommodation

At M'be, it seemed that every time agreement neared and the chiefs would pour their libations, the committee would change or a chief would be replaced. During the election campaign when Houphouet-Boigny was opening up to democracy, WARDA became a political punching bag. Nevertheless, some progress was made. The government had said that the original tract of 3000 hectares was too large and a process of cutting began that in several stages reduced the station to about a fourth of that. By 1990, agreement on 700 ha for WARDA had been reached and the boundaries marked, but the dispute with the villagers dragged on.

One factor in protracting the negotiations was the slowness of the government in making good on its promise to match the land lost to WARDA with comparable land nearby. When an understanding was reached with the farmers on replacing the lost land, another hitch developed. "The farmers would have to put in a lot more effort to clear the land. It was big work for them," says Chitti Babu Buyalla, who is head of farm management and engineering services at WARDA. So the farmers dug in their heels, says Chitti, as he is universally called. "The government did come to WARDA and said, "Look, we can compensate the property lost to the farmer, but we don't have the means to clear the land so the farmers can do that kind of cultivation. Can you assist us?' So WARDA said, 'Yes, please let us know how much land it will be.'"

WARDA's willingness to cooperate helped resolve that impasse. Then, just when final agreement appeared near, village representatives revived an old grievance. They complained that 3000 hectares had been taken from them some years before when the government established a forest reserve northwest of M'be. Now they insisted that they needed more land to make up for the loss of 360 hectares to WARDA. "The government demarked about 400 hectares of land in the forest and the ministry of agriculture requested that WARDA clear it. Land clearance went on for 3 or 4 years, and by the summer of 1996 only a few hectares remained to be cleared. "Our obligation is completed," said Chitti.

What was the effect on WARDA's research capabilities of this territorial wrangle? WARDA's objective was to retain land with enough ecological variety to permit the center to carry out work on the main rice growing systems in West Africa, says Matlon. "We're at about 80 percent of what would have all the scientists smiling all the time. The shortfall hasn't yet hurt our science significantly."

Farmers were still coming in through holes they cut in the fence and cultivating a few plots of maize and other crops on the WARDA farm. "We have to be a little bit patient with the farmers," said Chitti. "Since we are here anyway to help the farmers, we don't want to look like we are pushing them out of our land. Also, we want to have good neighborly relations. We have to live with them. That is our approach."

The Local Labor Market

Rice cultivation is very labor intensive and WARDA depends heavily on field workers recruited from the neighboring villages. Regular WARDA employees operate tractors and other machinery on the WARDA farm, but hundreds of villagers work as casual labor, the number varying according to the season and the work at hand.

At the start, many villagers were enthusiastic about working for WARDA, but reservations on the part of the government had to be overcome. The local *prefet* agreed with WARDA's argument that working there would make the villagers better farmers, but wanted to be certain that WARDA did not convert the villagers into daily wage earners at the cost of their ceasing to be food producing farmers. The matter was resolved when WARDA gave assurances that it would not monopolize workers' time during periods of peak labor need in local agriculture and would otherwise accommodate government concerns.

Training was essential because few people in the area had experience as rice farmers. Workers were trained in row planting and transplanting from the first year, but it took some time for them to become proficient. Chitti says that the pace of training could not be rushed. In the first season a handful of people were trained, in the second season 30. By 1993, WARDA had 60 trained workers. The overwhelming majority were men and a decision was made to encourage the hiring of women. Terry says that at first there was no particular push to recruit women but, when they scored well in work evaluations, an effort was made to increase the percentage of them in the work force. By

1997, women made up a quarter of the roughly 400 casual laborers who had been trained.

Normally, women farmed only for their families and did not work away from their villages. They were hesitant at first, says Chitti, but were attracted by the money since women were paid at the same rates as men. Following tradition, women at the start mostly did transplanting, some weeding and grain cleaning, while men did land preparation, fertilizer application and most of the weeding. Everyone took part in the harvest. Now women and men work in mixed groups and do the same work. Things are changing with some ramifications for the social structure, says Chitti, but it will take time.

Hazards Reduced

Basic first aid is available to workers. Any who suffer more serious accidents, which have been infrequent, are transported to Bouaké. Malaria is common, but was worse before an effective field drainage system was created ending the era when stagnant water covered the fields, providing a breeding ground for mosquitoes.

Then there are snakes. Several types of cobra and mamba are indigenous to the area. Certainly they posed a hazard when lowland areas at M'be were being developed and fish and frogs in the standing water were attractive quarry for reptiles. Workers are all issued boots, but Chitti says snakes do not currently present a serious problem since they generally shy away from human activity and there is plenty of space for them in uncleared land at M'be.

Among the reasons agricultural projects organized by outsiders in West Africa have typically been beset by labor problems is that such work may conflict with rural people's own farming activities or seem less rewarding than alternative employment in urban areas. So far, WARDA says it has not had problems with either numbers or the work ethic of field workers. A likely explanation is that earnings from WARDA have made a clear impact on the local economy. An unskilled worker in 1996 was paid 840 CFA francs or about $2 a day. Skilled workers earned 1260 and a top-level group, 1640. The pay is hardly munificent, but it is well above the legal minimum. By the standards of rural Africa, where opportunities for earning cash incomes are limited, WARDA pay makes a real difference in the villagers' ability to buy food and clothing, other basic consumer goods and, perhaps less fortunately, the beer that trucks now bring to villages in the area more frequently than in the pre-WARDA past.

Over the years, the dynamics of the WARDA-villager relationship have changed. The villagers no longer see WARDA simply as a group of outsiders coming in and driving them off their land. Now, WARDA is looked upon by many as an employer and even an ally. "We are working with the farmers," says Chitti, "The government administration is a little bit slow, they can't be forced. The farmers are depending on us to communicate their problems to the government. We are used by both sides. It's a triangular relationship."

The WARDA Farm

Land negotiations were a distraction but development of the WARDA "farm" proceeded even as the site was being whittled down to the ultimate 700 ha. Matlon said, "Every time we had to cut we tried to preserve the most representative soil for rice where you could do valid experimentation. We wanted to maintain as much of three valleys that are non-irrigated and as much of the irrigated portion as possible. It was a slimming exercise, so (the site) ended up following the shape of those valleys."

The three valleys Matlon mentions lie in a small watershed that gives M'be its name. WARDA was not the first to attempt to develop the area. Cotton had been grown at M'be as a commercial crop under a program run by a state company. Rice had also been cultivated there. In the 1970s, the government, with a rice production scheme in mind, constructed a dam to impound water from the stream to make irrigated farming possible on some 250 hectares downstream from the dam.

Defects in the original work at M'be and neglect in subsequent years left WARDA facing a formidable reclamation project. A major role in this task fell to Chitti Babu Buyalla, who had prime responsibility for farm development and management. According to Matlon, "Chitti's first job was to assess the old system and decide what was salvageable and what had to be reworked. But it was an awful irrigation system. I don't think the two feeder canals that run along the upper slopes had ever been used and they were completely clogged up. The farmers would send water through the drainage canal, which they would block up to flood the fields, so there was no drainage. It was enormously wasteful of water."

Chitti says that the irrigation system was "run by the farmers and supposed to be maintained by the farmers. Due to inadequacy of maintenance the whole system became unmanageable." The main problem was that "rice was a new crop for the farmers. They could not get the maximum benefit out of it. For example, they had cleared and were supposed to be cultivating over 200 hectares, but only about six hectares were under cultivation when we came. Most of the area was under elephant grass, and it was impossible to go in there even to walk. It was all inundated, unapproachable. It was difficult for farmers to cut because elephant grass is so hard, like sugar cane. So the farmers were really not using the system. There was just very nominal use here and there."

Water from the dam was also being used by farmers farther downstream. A few of these farmers came from Burkina Faso and Mali and knew something about cultivation under irrigated conditions. Some of the land was controlled by people in Bouaké and civil servants who had access to capital and equipment. But not more than 40 additional hectares were being worked, says Chitti. "The main reason was that the whole area was flooded. Because drains were not cleaned, canals not maintained, water from the dam not monitored, water had to go from field to field and the whole basin irrigated."

As work began on restoring the irrigation system, a master plan for the farm was being drawn up. A farm development committee was formed with research director Matlon as chairman, Chitti as secretary and all the scientists who would be using the land as members. "The idea was to find out their requirements and incorporate them into a plan to prepare the land properly for experimental use," says Chitti.

The major aim was to avoid the errors often made in setting up experiment stations in developing countries. Chitti says that there has been a tendency to choose more productive land and then improve it further by using deep tillage techniques and adding quantities of organic or chemical fertilizers. Land leveling, new roads and drains also change the character of these sites. Conditions on typical farms in West Africa are very different. When experiments done under improved conditions are moved to farmers' fields, says Chitti, "we find always a big gap from the result obtained (on the research station). Technology transfer is not an easy thing."

Simulating Slash and Burn

At M'be, a decision was made to develop the farm to reflect three levels of management—low- medium- and high-input. Low-input management would be similar to the traditional slash and burn system used by West African farmers. When farmers clear their upland fields, "they cut only the bush and leave the stumps of big trees because of the work required to remove them. The vegetation is burned," says Chitti. "The moment the rains come they use the hand hoe for plowing, breaking the clods and smoothing the earth. Then they sow the field by dribbling or broadcasting seed. No fertilizers or insecticides are used." Plots would be weeded a maximum of two or three times during the growing season. In recent years, farmers cultivated such fields for perhaps three years then let them lie fallow for five or six, says Chitti. "It used to be more, and now, because of land pressure, the fallow period is being cut to even three years. Some farmers are using land continuously. The yields are getting bad."

According to Matlon, the major aim of the low-input management protocols was to preserve the original quality of the land. At research stations elsewhere, scientists had been given the freedom to apply any sort of inputs or management they wished. This included land leveling, deep plowing and applying atypical levels of fertilizer, The result has been that, over time, the fundamental nature of the soil was changed. And at some point the process could not be reversed. Technology was being screened on soils that were no longer representative of farmers' conditions. The results, inevitably, were not like results obtained outside the fence.

WARDA decided to preserve a major share—about 40 percent—of cropland at M'be, under conditions that were truly typical of poor farmers' experience. To do that, maximums were established for inputs with the levels set low enough to avoid long-term residual effects on the soil. The rules prescribed very shallow plowing and no application of herbicides or pesticides. Limited application of nitrogen was allowed because it leaves the soil after a time. Initial clearing was done by hand in the way the farmers do to avoid compacting the soil by use of heavy equipment. WARDA also emulates the fallow periods used by upland farmers, a practice that requires that a lot of land be idle and is a reason that the WARDA farm has to be as large as it is.

In another sector at M'be, amounting to 20 to 25 percent of land used for experiments, researchers are free to do high-input experiments. High-input management on the farm amounts to "classical research station management," says Chitti. "We would do deep tillage if needed by the scientist, provide high doses of fertilizer, land leveling, whatnot. We can maintain pesticide-free areas, herbicide-free areas. All of this falls into the pattern of intensive farming done in industrial countries."

Another zone is devoted to medium input management. This would describe the approach of a progressive farmer in West Africa. Such a farmer uses animal traction and small power tillage equipment and probably applies some fertilizer and pesticides, at least for crops for which there is a market. While there are some practitioners of high-input agriculture in the region, around 80 percent of farmers use low-input management, says Chitti. "I don't know the figures exactly, but my guess is that medium input is 19 percent and high input one percent."

With WARDA's farm divided into low-, medium- and high-input areas and threshold levels set, scientists provide the protocols for land and input requirements they want for an experiment, says Chitti, "A crop map for the year is drawn up. The land is prepared for them and the scientists come and do their planting and take their result. I maintain the field history."

Much of the M'be site was deliberately left in its original state, said Terry in his last year as DG. "We decided that, apart from the places where we were going to develop physical structures, we were not going to have any mass clearing of land. We would clear land only as we required it and we wanted a lot of original benchmark sites, reference points, so that we can always come back and see what are the characteristics of the soil, the vegetation and so forth where it had not been cleared, as opposed to what we'd cleared to do experiments. Of the total 700 hectares we have probably not cleared more than 50 percent, plus the 40 hectares or so we had to clear for the actual physical installations. So we have a lot of uncleared land. Under 100 ha is currently under cultivation."

Getting Started at M'be

When the new WARDA began operating in Côte d'Ivoire in 1988, headquarters was a villa in the Kennedy residential quarter of Bouaké. Management, finance and personnel sections were accommodated there. But a push was made to get research started at M'be and some rough prefabs were rapidly erected. Terry says the prefabs were the idea of board member Ronnie Coffman who recalled that Nobelist Norman Borlaug got started in Mexico with something very similar to the shed-like buildings put up at M'be. "This is where you would normally keep seed and fertilizer. We made them into labs and got going. We said the fancy stuff will come later. So people were impressed. We were getting work started as fast as possible at the M'be site."

Plans for the "fancy stuff" in the form of permanent facilities for the new WARDA were being discussed even before the move to Bouaké. Terry says he had been pointed toward a firm of architects in England, Norman and Dawbarn, by Les Swindale, then director general of the International Crops Research Institute for the Semi-Arid Tropics. ICRISAT had recently had the experience of developing a major installation in Africa with its Sahelian center in Niger. Terry says that when he went to the firm and described what he had in mind, he was advised "to hire a development officer who was also an architect. He could help WARDA's leaders think through what they wanted up to the stage of asking for tenders for architectural services, etc."

Peter Mather, a British architect with experience in Africa, joined WARDA in Monrovia as development officer and work on a concept began. Terry opted against the model of some CGIAR centers that are fairly grand complexes and create a jarring first world contrast with their third world settings. Terry says he told Mather, "I think for a center like this you need to get away from the kind of architecture that is very marbley and modern with sealed windows. Get away from that. Get as close to nature as possible."

"Based on that we began to put the concept on paper and developed what we called the design scheme. Then we put it out to tender. Norman and Dawbarn, not surprisingly, won. They had shown interest at the beginning and had sent this man who worked for them. It was not bias, I can tell you that. A lot of architectural firms bid for it, and their bid just turned out to be the best. Then we started to look for the money, for donors who would be willing to pay for the design drawings and for the original architectural work to be done." WARDA soon found that it faced an uphill fight in raising construction funds.

The late 1980s was an inopportune time for WARDA to mobilize financial support. The CGIAR budget was under pressure and other centers were being forced to trim staff and programs in the downsizing style of the period. Donors were particularly reluctant to finance capital projects which, of course, put a crimp in WARDA's plans. Curt Farrar, the CGIAR executive secretary then, recalls that WARDA's stock with donors had not recovered. When he and TAC chairman Guy Camus were called on to explain the plan to relaunch WARDA and rally support for it, the donors displayed a distinct lack of enthusiasm. "A large part of what Guy and I had to do was to convince the donors to give it a chance to work."

"Initially the donors were very cool," says Terry. "Some told us outright, don't introduce the matter of bricks and mortar. We're not interested. Well, we argued that, hey, one of the things that make us very weak is that we don't have a home. The fact that WARDA was in a six-story building, in which it only had two floors anyway, in the middle of Monrovia, did not give it a good image. It was not a credible center.

Cutting a Compromise

"A few donors said OK, you need a home. If you don't have one you're just going to disappear. We quickly narrowed it to about 5 or 6 donors who were willing to put money into bricks and mortar. They were Japan, Germany, Canada, Netherlands, France and the African Development Bank. Of course, we tried to interest the member states to be part of that donor group and they made all kinds of pledges, but that didn't come to pass.

"It involved a lot of travel for us, sensitizing people, explaining plans to them, showing how the strategy was going, how the recruitment was going. They were receptive, but cautiously so, because this was an organization that had a lot of baggage. Donors had to satisfy themselves that this was a new WARDA. The Netherlands took the responsibility to convene donor meetings and the CGIAR Secretariat provided some logistic support. Curt Farrar backed us up saying, 'These guys know what they are doing, they are starting to develop some very interesting ideas. If they can come up with concrete plans we would like to encourage you to consider support for them.'"

WARDA planners completed a design scheme and a cost estimate and prepared to present them to the donors. Although the plan was modest in scale by CGIAR standards the encounter with the donors brought a rude awakening. The plan called for a three-phase building program, says Terry. "Phase 1 was the research phase. Phase 2 would have been training and documentation and a library. Phase 3 would have been administration. It was supposed to cost us about $20 million for everything."

A meeting with prospective donors was arranged and Terry remembers that before the meeting Curt Farrar warned them to be "very careful, because the dynamics were very interesting. The donors are likely to follow the lead of the first person who speaks. If he comes out very positive and passionate they will follow. If he comes out negative then woe betide you.

"I remember after we put the proposition out, the first to take the floor was France who said it was just too big. Try to do something about it. It continued that way around the table. I remember the Japanese representative at that time, he didn't talk very much, but when they were going round the table asking people for their reactions, 'Too big.' Then we asked, can you give us some guidelines? Somebody then said if you go in a modular form where you can be building it by bits, pack as much as you can into the first module, and if you can keep that to about $10 million we'll try to support you.

"We came back and did some work to see how many things we can pack into this first phase. We managed on paper to come up with the $10 million. But eventually it cost $12 million. We did not put in the cost of farm development, the cost of infrastructure—roads, culverts, that sort of thing. And, also, the lab furnishings. The $10 million was just to build the structure, the extra $2 million was for those other things."

Terry says that Japan, the Netherlands and France immediately put money on the table and before long WARDA had $3 million to $4 million pledged. Before it signed a contract WARDA wanted to have $6 million securely in hand. There were encouraging signs that France and the Netherlands were disposed to make further substantial contributions. Either would bring the kitty up to the $6-million mark. Terry recalls a memorable WARDA board meeting "in which the board said you tell us what you want us to do in terms of giving the authority to move. We said give us the authority to move provided that during centers week meeting France or the Netherlands announces its pledge."

A Tremendous Gamble

At centers week, however, the hopes placed in both were dashed. "With the Dutch," says Terry, "the man we negotiated with and who had convened the very first donor meeting had left the science research part of the ministry of foreign affairs. He was supposed to have briefed the person who was taking over about these pledges. Well, he didn't, so when we met with the guy, there was I talking with somebody who didn't know anything about it."

In the case of France, "Somebody had told them that we were not collaborating with CORAF *(Conférence des responsables de la recherche agronomique africaine)*," says Terry. CORAF had been formed in the middle 1980s under French auspices to promote regional cooperation in agricultural research. Terry says that CORAF expressed a desire to collaborate with WARDA and "We said OK, we are ready, we will go to your meetings, provide all kinds of information, etc., but for some reason, somebody had told people in the cooperation division of the ministry of foreign affairs that WARDA was not cooperating with CORAF and therefore WARDA was not cooperating with national programs." And they said, "So with this now, we are in no position to (pay) the pledge.

"When we got these two bits of bad news, we sat down and pondered what we were going to do. The board says we can go and sign the contract provided the French and Netherlands honor their pledges. WARDA's financial officer Gordon MacNeil went to Ottawa to talk to a Canadian member of the WARDA board telling him that two major donors were keeping WARDA in limbo and not giving the needed assurances on funding. The board member's reaction was, in effect, 'you cannot sign the contract,'" says Terry. He was "very skeptical about the prudence and wisdom of moving on the contract."

"Still, it was management's decision, having received the board's go ahead. So we agonized, agonized about it, and we all decided if we let this drop now we will have to start from scratch, we'll even have to give some of this money back. I did contact the board chairman and told him what had happened, that my gut feeling was to go with it.

"We had this meeting, all the members of the WARDA executive management committee. It was somewhat foolhardy, but we decided to go with it. I went to Abidjan and signed the contract. We had about $5 million. The very next day I got a telex from the chairman saying he had received a letter from the Canadian board member who said it would be a tremendous gamble if we were to sign the contract. As far as he, the chairman, was concerned he still stuck to his recommendation, but once a board member put in writing that it was a gamble the chairman now said it was his duty to stop us. So I said, We have signed the contract." There was a fair amount of drama.

"We regrouped again and said what are we going to do? There was only one thing to do. The DG started begging again. People started saying, you're fairly diligent. Let's see what happens. They said we'll support you if you go for a line of credit from Citibank. Get the CGIAR Secretariat to write a letter of support saying that prospects of WARDA continuing to receive donor support were good. We did that and we got the line."

"With the money from Citibank we were able to meet our cash-flow commitments. Then we started with donors to develop a plan on how to pay the debt." A 3-year repayment plan was developed starting at the end of 1992. The Netherlands came through. Their new man in the post of donor representative had learned about WARDA, actually had visited WARDA. "Germany, Canada, Japan all said we will help pay the debt," said Terry. It was paid off on schedule in 1995. "Right to the last penny it has been paid. That's a source of joy to me. In fact, we had a little left over to pay the architect to do the drawings for Phase 2."

Hard Bargaining

While negotiations with donors went on, WARDA had found a contractor to build a scaled-down $10 million center. Under Peter Mather's coaching, WARDA aimed for a fixed cost contract. Because of West Africa's economic troubles, "It was a buyers market," says Terry, "and a construction company in Abidjan with a good reputation was willing to accept such a contract." It took hard bargaining, but the parties finally agreed on a deal WARDA could afford and the company was prepared to accept. "They said, 'We can do it for $10 million,'" says Terry, 'but you will have to come up with a cash flow plan to make sure that, at a given moment, the money is there. If that does not take place, the penalty is yours.' In other words, as long as (WARDA) was able to maintain our end of the bargain, OK. But if there were any delays or there were extra costs we bore those costs." So WARDA signed what amounted to a turnkey contract.

WARDA also had to cope with the ordinary complications of doing business in Africa. Gordon MacNeil identifies three issues that were very important in the business affairs of WARDA—the currency question, WARDA's tax status, and the problem of customs and logistics at Abidjan's port and airport.

The currency problem had a unique West African twist. The CFA franc was a hard currency supported by the French treasury, but there were strong intimations that support would be withdrawn and a severe devaluation would occur. WARDA, therefore, avoided keeping large sums in CFA deposits. This resulted in constant difficulties in transferring funds into Côte d'Ivoire and through Abidjan banks, but when devaluation did come in 1994 WARDA was not heavily exposed.

Customs operations are a notorious bottleneck in West African countries. Delay is endemic, theft not unusual and bribery customary. With lots of machinery and scientific equipment scheduled to be imported by WARDA, difficulties with customs could have dire effects. WARDA took a direct and pragmatic approach. Customs and foreign ministry officials and others in positions to affect shipments to WARDA were invited to Bouaké for a day. They were given red carpet treatment, shown M'be, and WARDA's work was explained in detail. They were told that they would be important partners in the endeavor and would be proud of the result. It worked. According to MacNeil, cooperation was exemplary and he knew of nothing untoward happening at WARDA'S expense at the docks or airport.

Another potentially serious problem was WARDA's tax status. Under the country agreement signed with Côte d'Ivoire, WARDA was exempt from all taxes except a value added tax (VAT) on goods and services. VAT in Côte d'Ivoire was set at a whopping 25 percent. An exception had been granted in the case of WARDA's building program. The catch was that WARDA would be required to pay the VAT and then have it reimbursed. The government was under heavy financial pressure at the time and there was no realistic expectation that the money would be refunded in a timely way.

There was an out, however, an arrangement under which the government could issue vouchers defraying future tax liability in the amounts paid. WARDA argued that it simply did not have the estimated $2.5 million required to go the refund route and proposed that its contractor accept the tax credits to be set off against WARDA payments. The company, a large, successful and aggressive firm, did a volume of business in the country large enough to make such an arrangement viable, but resisted vigorously. Finally, after much wrangling and with a push from the ministry of finance, the company accepted the terms. The alternative, WARDA said, was that it would cancel the contract.

First Phase Revised

The three-phase construction program called for in the original master plan for WARDA's headquarters and main research center would have created a sprawling complex of buildings connected by covered walkways to protect against sun and rain. A large laboratory and office building was to be built in the first phase. Separate structures for a library and documentation center, administration wing, and cafeteria and conference center were scheduled to follow. In all, there were plans for some 17 buildings including a farm workshop, farm office building and facilities for storage and other services. The cost would have been $20 million plus for the physical plant alone.

As modified under the $10 million dispensation, the research building, in addition to laboratories and offices for scientists, holds the offices of the director general, director of research and director of training as well as of other top administrative officers. Other buildings include an insectarium adjacent to the main research building, a workshop where mechanical repairs are made, housing for a backup electric generator, and minor structures like that for security guards.

The limits on funding had forced a radical scaling back of the building program. "By modifying the plan we had to sacrifice and had to compromise," says Terry. "First of all, if we are going to be a viable commodity improvement center we should have had our own genetic resources conservation facility. Cold storage, long term storage, containment facility, moisture control, all of that."

WARDA had a collection of more than 10,000 rice accessions, the majority of which were duplicated by either IITA or IRRI, but space to house a larger collection in more sophisticated facilities was in the original blueprint for the WARDA research building. When the donor that WARDA hoped would finance the genebank did not come through, an empty place was left for it when the research building was constructed, the "bare shell" space representing a hope for the future. Pressure for lab space mounted, however, and then, says Terry, "IITA came knocking on the door. They said, 'We like what's going on here, you've got a good facility. We're going to be moving into the moist savanna. We know this is the transition zone, but you have as much humid forest here as you have savanna and we think we'd like to be based in Bouaké. We need a facility here.'" Since WARDA has full access to IITA's genebank and WARDA's lowland rice research program is quartered at IITA, a quid pro quo was indicated. "So we converted what was to have become our genebank to the facility that we gave to IITA," says Terry. WARDA did have adequate short term seed storage in one of the prefab buildings at M'be and was able to keep a working collection of germplasm there.

A library had been started in WARDA's temporary headquarters in Bouaké, but it was clear that having the library in Bouaké and the scientists at M'be was unsatisfactory. "We converted a fertilizer shed and seed store to a documentation center and library. For what used to be a seed shed, we are very proud of it." The library's collection of books and journals is not impressive, but WARDA's documentalist, Alassane Diallo, has developed computerized access to external sources to a degree that makes the WARDA facility probably the most useful agricultural science library in the region. It is used by NARS researchers as well as WARDA staff.

Running Out of Space

Terry says that it quickly became evident that research needs were going to overrun the space available. "And we did, even though we built that monstrosity out there, which was supposed to be a stores building." The monstrosity Terry refers to is a gracelessly utilitarian two-story building standing near the motor pool at some distance from the research building.

Chitti, who has been in the thick of things at every stage in the development of the M'be site recalls that, "In '94, we realized that our program was developing fast and our research facilities were not adequate. New programs were coming in and had to be lodged. Also, storage was one of the biggest problems. We said let us build with the small funds available a central stores building, use $60,000 to build it. Then, since we were under pressure, we said OK, all the farm and the administration (functions) should be moved out of the research building so that we can accommodate scientists there. Let us add some offices in the stores building. That is the reason we now have 24 offices there with space for stores behind. It was completed in March '95."

A deep well and water tower provide trustworthy drinking water and a microwave tower affords links for moderately sophisticated communications. A road had to be built from the highway, which is about 8 kms from the entrance to the WARDA farm. In all, about 40 kms of road have been constructed on the M'be site. WARDA did not have the money to tarmac any of these roads, so maintenance work must be done constantly, particularly in the rainy season.

A substantial part of WARDA's investment at M'be doesn't show. For example, a decision was made to spend some $300,000 of scarce resources on a backup generator. Electricity is brought in to M'be from the national grid, also about 8 kms. away, and the power supply in Côte d'Ivoire is considerably more reliable than in many West African countries. But it was thought prudent to insure that electricity would flow to the labs and seed storage facility should regular service be interrupted.

Infrastructure limitations in Côte d'Ivoire as well as WARDA's tight funds delayed the installation at M'be of some technology now common in other CGIAR centers. WARDA's budget stretched to purchase of personal computers for the staff, but was inadequate to buy the hardware and software necessary to connect them in a network and pay the personnel to operate it. However, the headquarters building was wired for a network when it was built, since it was much less expensive to do it during construction than in a retrofit. In part because of WARDA's dependence on a microwave link to Bouaké for telecommunications, access to e-mail was limited for several years to an awkward centralized system. In 1997, long-term planning paid off when a network and individual e-mail access became operational.

As for food service, Chitti says that in the early days staff members brought their own food to M'be. "The staff grew larger and we needed dining facilities. We were getting continuous visitors and its not practical to take them to Bouaké for lunch and lose more than 2 hours. Also we needed a gathering place for staff to interact, etc. Originally there was a plan for a closed cafeteria. We estimated about $200,000 just for the cafeteria, and we don't have that kind of money."

A Local Effort

At the site of the original WARDA buildings at M'be, dubbed the upland center, Chitti had overseen construction of a small open structure with local materials and in African style. Designed and constructed for $3000, it was used as a conference center, for training classes and for seminars. "For our climate it was very appropriate. Says Chitti, "We said, this is a good idea, let us do the same thing (for a dining facility). So I designed it to hold about 150 people, also, with an adjacent kitchen facility. We opted to look around, get local materials, use free ventilation. Notice, when you close buildings under tropical conditions, put in air conditioning, there's a lot of mold, fungus. Then they stink inside, contribute to a big maintenance problem."

The dining hall, known as the apatam, the word for hut or structure in a local language, is situated on a rise perhaps a hundred meters from the research building. The view out across the valley through the open sides is agreeable and the thatched roof and what Chitti calls the "tunneling effect" of air moving up the slope keeps temperatures tolerable even on M'be's frequent very steamy days. "We chose a nice looking site and after discussion we agreed and built it for about $24,000. It was done all by our own people—design, building, everything, furniture included. We gave them the contract, provided materials. Thatching was done by people from Bouaké whose forefathers were from Burkina Faso. It should go about 20 years. Maybe more."

Still absent was a training center. The prefab buildings were used for training, but the facilities were minimal compared with those of other CGIAR centers. Most of the CGIAR commodity research centers have living accommodations for people who attend training programs and for visitors. Chitti says the decision not to invest in them was also based on cost considerations. He says it is less expensive to bus trainees out from Bouaké rather than spend on security and a variety of other services at M'be.

In appearance, WARDA's headquarters at M'be seems to owe less to indigenous architecture than Terry originally may have had in mind. In style, the one-story headquarters building has an unassertive functional look, although the light colored metal roof was designed to suggest the lines of African thatched roofs. In scale, compared to other CGIAR research centers, the WARDA headquarters is more modest than monumental. The scientists' laboratories and offices are housed in two parallel wings. These are connected by sections holding offices so that the structure is formed around grassy courtyards. The offices and labs are air conditioned, but the corridors are open.

The architect, Jim Hunter, advocated brick construction for reasons of both aesthetics and durability. This posed a problem because Côte d'Ivoire had no brickworks and no bricklayers. Bricks were purchased in neighboring Burkina Faso and brought in by train on the national railroad that runs a few kilometers from the M'be gate. Burkinabe bricklayers were recruited for the job and in turn trained a cadre of Ivorians. There was a period when a few of the walls built by the neophyte bricklayers had to be redone, but the Ivorians rapidly developed journeyman skills. Apparently because the design was unfamiliar, workmanship also became a factor in construction of the metal roof. In hard downpours buckets sometimes had to be deployed in the corridors because of leaks. A warranty on the building obliges the contractor to fix such faults.

On the major counts of plan and equipment, the laboratories seem to score well. Visiting scientists rank the labs at M'be with the best among international research centers. Matlon and others say that the key was the architect's willingness to interact with scientists to learn their needs and preferences and to keep revising plans until they were satisfied that the design was right. A virtue of the design is the flexibility that permits labs to be converted into offices rapidly and vice versa at low cost if requirements change.

Another Threat to Survival

The new WARDA plant had been completed on schedule and within budget and, when it was occupied in 1992, it seemed a symbol of hard-earned stability and permanence. But very soon thereafter the center was confronted with its most serious challenge since the debate over its survival in the middle 1980s. Many in the CGIAR remained skeptical toward a center devoted exclusively to a single crop in one region. There was also growing concern at the time that rice yields were not increasing at a rate sufficient to meet future demand and the CGIAR's Technical Advisory Committee (TAC) initiated a broad review of both research and budget policies on rice.

WARDA mounted a successful defense. The key argument was that CGIAR planning should not focus narrowly on its own research. WARDA urged that the group take a broader view, consider the investment in rice research by other organizations as well as in its own centers and, thereby, put the CGIAR effort into a true global perspective. "That was not orthodox at that time," says Matlon. "Now it's the essential thing, that we're part of the global system. That is the new religion. We tried to open it up and do the congruence analysis properly." The incident also spurred on WARDA efforts to refine the practice of rice economics in West Africa. (See Appendix).

The discussion contributed to a significant change in how the CGIAR sees itself in relation to the global agricultural research system. WARDA emerged from the review with TAC's blessing on its budget and a tacit endorsement of its regional character. The group went along with what TAC advised, and in doing so affirmed that the CGIAR regarded WARDA and West Africa as forming a special case.

Chitti Babu Buyalla

Chitti is a product of the international agricultural research system that developed after World War II. He earned a degree in agricultural engineering and technology from Orissa University in India in the late 1960s and was channeled into international work when he was picked for a Rockefeller Foundation-sponsored program to train people to develop and manage agricultural research stations in India. Rockefeller was heavily engaged in institution building in Asia in the 1950s and 1960s and the idea of the program was to change the way research stations were organized and run.

The conventional pattern in India was for research stations to be at least partly self-financing. "The idea normally was that production was supposed to be profitable and the funds raised from production should be invested for research. Experience taught that when research and production are combined in a station, usually the research operations are affected in a negative sense," says Chitti. "Production means money, so you have a production man in charge. There are external pressures and the whole thing is unbalanced on the production side."

"The biggest problem arising from the divided mission is that the land is not used properly," says Chitti. "The interests are different" and the layout of the experiments and other activities conflict. "Production people don't respect the rotation methods and other things. They are interested in having a very good crop. They may dump in fertilizer to get a higher yield, but that may not be the objective of the researchers.

"It creates a lot of problems for researchers. Their requirements are entirely different. Researchers need more precision." To serve scientists' objectives it is necessary to develop a station to carry experiments exclusively, "so we can monitor the operation and maintain the field history." A field history is a permanent record of crops planted, chemicals used, etc., in specific areas. "In future, if there is a problem on the farm we can find out whether it is the farm's problem, or a management problem."

Chitti clearly embraced this theory of how a research station should be developed, organized and operated. Through much of his career he has practiced it, spending a lot of time developing new stations and managing them mostly under the aegis of CGIAR centers. In 1971 he was employed in one of the early Rockefeller backed projects supporting research station development in India and also got his first experience working with rice. In 1974 he joined the CGIAR's newly formed International Center for Research for the Semi-Arid Tropics as a research station development engineer as ICRISAT established its headquarters and research center near Hyderabad. In his five years with ICRISAT in India, he worked as a farm manager and was loaned out to assist Indian universities, which were developing research stations in collaboration with ICRISAT.

In 1980 he went to Tanzania as farm manager in a joint CIMMYT-ICRISAT-IITA program at the national food crop research institute. After a side trip to act as a consultant in Bulawayo he moved on to Zaire in 1984 to work for IITA on the national manioc program sponsored by USAID in Shaba province about 200 km from Kinshasa. There again he was farm manager and responsible for station development. Then, in July of 1990 he joined WARDA.

WARDA campus at M'be before expansion in late 1990's. Headquarters and labs are in main building at top left. Backup generator is in structure at center. Small building (top center) is insectarium. Apatam and kitchen are at top right.

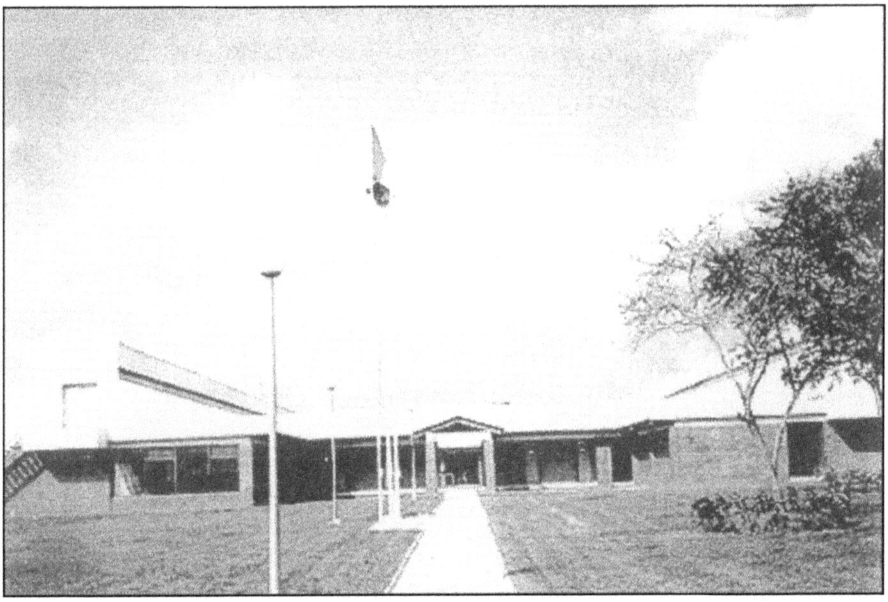

Front entrance of WARDA headquarters and main research center at M'Be.

Soil science laboratory is typical of space at the M´be research building that is designed to be readily convertible as office or laboratory space for scientists.

Open-sided dining and meeting facility (apatam) was built of local materials.

3 Wide Crossing

A New Direction

The new WARDA set its top priority on benefiting West Africa's rice farmers who grow their crops under rainfed conditions. Irrigated rice would not be ignored, but WARDA's main effort and major resources would be aimed at helping the greater number who farm in the "upland\inland valley continuum." While the new direction was proclaimed in the center's strategic plan, the practical details of how to implement it were still lacking.

This began to change with the arrival in 1991 of new rice breeders for the center's upland, lowland and irrigated rice programs. The upland rice breeder was Monty Patrick Jones, a Sierra Leone national who came to WARDA from heading a cooperative rice research program in Cameroon funded by USAID and implemented by IITA. Jones had previously led a team that bred mangrove rice varieties that are now widely used in West Africa in that production system. He was, therefore, someone who had already succeeded in developing improved rice varieties compatible with African conditions.

The three breeders reached WARDA at about the same time, says Jones. "We first read the literature to find out about the state of development and production. That's when we got the first shock. We found that after three to four decades of rice variety improvement work in West Africa, the majority of upland farmers in the region are holding on to traditional varieties. We had a problem," says Jones. "We had to find out why these farmers are not utilizing the new varieties."

He notes that rainfed production systems probably occupied as much as 80 percent of the area devoted to rice production in West Africa. These areas were mainly cultivated by farmers who practiced traditional agriculture and who did not have the resources to purchase external inputs like fertilizer, herbicides and insecticides. And even when they used them, they usually did not apply the optimal doses, says Jones. "These are the people who had been neglected."

Rice breeding programs in West Africa had focused on developing varieties for so-called improved management. Almost all the testing of these varieties was done on research stations where land preparation was good and external inputs were applied. "It is not surprising that varieties developed under these conditions and then taken to the farmers' situation did not perform well at all." says Jones. "Farmers held on to the traditional varieties." Jones sees no blame due the previous WARDA breeders since the center's mandate was to import rice varieties from outside the region and determine how they fared in West African conditions. Until about 1985 very little work had been done on screening for what breeders call location-specific stresses.

The WARDA breeders made their analysis and proceeded to lay out a program. Jones says that in his own case, he had a good idea of the direction to take but did not go it alone. He had discussions with national leaders and scientists so that "it was clear what each country was looking for. Then we drew up a program that was aimed at the things that had been left out."

Focus on Soil and Weeds

In Jones's domain of upland rice production, very little research had been done on traditional cultivation systems. With such low-input systems, two major problems have to be considered. First, soil nutrients are inadequate and farmers do not make up for it by applying fertilizers. Second, with use of land in each successive year, weed infestation increases. Biological stresses like drought and plant diseases such as blast strike periodically, but nutrient depletion and weeds are always there. It is because of these constants that upland farmers must practice slash and burn farming, cultivating the land for a few years then moving on.

Previously, breeders had largely neglected low-input farmers and concentrated on improved management systems. For the upland areas, WARDA's new policy was to breed for low-, medium-, and high-input systems simultaneously. Because of past neglect, the new emphasis was on the low- and medium-input systems. In addition to the attention to low-input farming, grain quality was given high priority. Jones says that sometimes in the past, at a fairly late stage of development of an improved variety, "farmers might say 'I don't want this material because it doesn't look like rice. It looks like maize.' This happened in Côte d'Ivoire where we went into a community to test a good, high-yielding material, but they said 'We want rice not maize and rejected it.' So we had to develop varieties with appropriate grain qualities."

To attain the goal of helping poor rice farmers produce beyond the subsistence level it was necessary to come up with a rice plant that would not only offer increased yields and withstand the climate, plant diseases and pests of the region, but also have qualities acceptable to West African consumers. The challenge was clear, but the way to meet it was not.

Hidden Potential

When Jones and his fellow WARDA plant breeders reviewed rice research in West Africa he says that it was evident that not much had been done "to exploit the potential of the traditional, indigenous germplasm." Rice was domesticated in Africa at least 3500 years ago and an indigenous type, *Oryza glaberrima*, is one of only two species of rice cultivated seriously out of a score of species known worldwide. But *glaberrima* has been largely displaced from farmers' fields on its home ground of West Africa by *Oryza sativa* from Asia, which was introduced to Africa about 500 years ago, presumably by traders from Asia and the Middle East.

Jones notes that *O. Sativa* has three distinct subtypes, japonica from East Asia, indica from the Indian subcontinent and javanica from south Asia. The javanicas never took hold in Africa. The indicas adapted well to lowland growing conditions and more than 90 percent of lowland materials in West Africa are indicas. A similar percentage of rice grown in upland conditions are japonicas, now known as tropical japonicas.

What accounts for the popularity of the *sativas* is superior yield; they produce substantially more rice per plant than the *glaberrimas*. The difference is in the conformation of the plants. The Asian import has secondary branches in the grain-bearing panicles while the African plant typically lacks such secondary branches. Jones says that at the point where a single rice grain may be attached to a primary branch of a *glaberrima* plant, a *sativa* plant will have a secondary branch with three, four or five grains attached. The indigenous plant not only produces fewer grains per plant, but has an unfortunate tendency to lodge (fall over) and shatter (shed grains). Also, many *glaberrimas* produce red rice. West Africans generally prefer white rice, says Jones. "These are disadvantages that we have to overcome."

Not all the virtues, however, are on the *sativa* side. Many *glaberrima* types are stoutly drought tolerant and, best of all for upland conditions, compete well with weeds. The plant does so primarily because it grows rapidly at the seedling stage, is relatively tall and bushy and has droopy leaves that shade out the weeds. It is also known for good taste and aroma, which largely explains why farmers still grow it for their own use despite the lower yields.

West African farmers had been doing their own crop improvement work on rice for centuries by saving seeds from their best rice plants at harvest time and sowing them the next season. However, rice research in the modern fashion was begun in the region in the 1920s and 1930s by both British and French colonial governments. The work concentrated on selection and breeding of *O. Sativa* and the introduction of new varieties from outside Africa. Research activity picked up in the 1950s and, in particular, France's institute for tropical agricultural research (IRAT) worked to develop *sativa* varieties adapted to African conditions. In the 1970s, the CGIAR's International Institute of Tropical Agriculture (IITA) began doing rice research. It preceded WARDA in carrying out varietal improvement work and scored some successes, notably in increasing yields in irrigated varieties.

In the years that followed, research for the most part benefited irrigated rice and swamp rice. Since those ecosystems accounted for a relatively small proportion of the rice grown in West Africa the effect on total production was modest. None of the postwar research programs produced material that was clearly better for upland cultivation. Little research was done on *O.Glaberrima*. With the demand for rice and the cost of rice imports both rising rapidly, West African governments in the 1960s began asking international development agencies to underwrite massive water control projects to increase the area of irrigated cropland in the region. WARDA was created outside the CGIAR in this period on the model of the International Rice Research Institute (IRRI) in the Philippines in the hope that WARDA would do for West Africa what IRRI was doing for Asia. WARDA in its early years continued on the well-trodden path of evaluating imported rice types and trying to adapt them.

Reclaiming Glaberrima

Jones says that when the new WARDA plant breeders looked back on the previous three or four decades it was clear that "We've made very limited gains because japonica has a limited level of resistance to some of the major stresses we have, to blast disease, drought, acidity, salinity. You can't go beyond a threshold level of resistance." *Glaberrima*, on the other hand, has "developed protective mechanisms that enable it to resist major stresses. It has good resistance to blast, to drought, to acidity, to the rice yellow mottle virus, and it has other resistances which we don't have to date in *sativa*. So it was decided that *glaberrima* had to be exploited somehow."

Prospects did not appear bright. Attempts had been made earlier to "improve" *glaberrima* by crossing it with rice varieties from elsewhere, but these had not prospered. Jones says that "a major problem why *glaberrima* has not been exploited is the fact that when you cross it with *sativa* you wind up with sterile progeny. We believe that it is controlled by a recessive gene and that is a serious problem."

Finding *glaberrimas* that would lend themselves to the breeding endeavor meant drawing on the pool of germplasm available. With the use of *sativa* spreading, the supply of *glaberrima* germplasm was being rapidly eroded as farmers abandoned the indigenous species. "Fortunately," says Jones, "there had been several collecting missions in West Africa. They started in the '60s with a group of Japanese scientists who came into the region and, maybe for academic purposes, wanted to collect African germplasm. A good number of *Oryza glaberrima* and other types were collected. We had good reports on the morphology, cytology, etc., of these materials. After that, a number of collecting missions were carried out in West Africa by some national programs and by French scientists. Other institutions, including the CGIAR's International Plant Genetic Resources Institute (IPGRI) and WARDA also organized collecting missions.

When WARDA's genebank at Fendall in Liberia was destroyed in the civil war the loss of *glaberrima* germplasm stored there could have been disastrous. Luckily, duplicate samples of most of these materials had been sent to IITA so that WARDA was able to recoup. Jones says that currently WARDA has some 16,000 germplasm samples in its collection at M'be of which about 1,500 are *glaberrima.*

Collection and conservation of genetic materials was only the beginning of the job. The next step was to characterize the *glaberrima* samples. Characterizing rice varieties involves a painstaking process of growing them and carefully observing and recording important attributes in order to know what traits captured in the genes can be exploited in future crosses. In the case of the neglected *glaberrimas*, Jones says the results were surprising and encouraging. "We produced catalogues of all the materials we characterized for *glaberrima*," says Jones. "These catalogues turned out to be very important. In fact, it was that initial characterization that led us to say, yes, we can exploit the *glaberrima*." This opened the way to creation of the Wide Crossing program aimed at hybridizing *sativa* and *glaberrima*. "We characterized the 1500 *glaberrimas* in our collection for a range of morphological traits and for their reaction to normal stresses," says Jones. "The morphological characterization was very, very interesting because we found out that, contrary to previous belief, the growth durations within the *glaberrimas* compare well with what we have in the *sativas*. For example, in some *glaberrimas* the range from the minimum to maximum is more than what you have in the *sativa*. We have *glaberrimas* that would mature in 60 days from sowing. At the other extreme, we found varieties that would mature in 150, 160 days. For most *sativa* types the minimum is about 90 days to maturity. So this is one trait of *glaberrima* that we can exploit. In drought-affected areas these quick maturing materials are desirable because rice can be grown to maturity during even a short rainy season.

"When it comes to the number of panicles, we found that, contrary to belief, the number of panicles, not spikelets but panicles, in many of the *glaberrima* materials is much, much higher than in the *sativa*. Even when we compared the number of panicles within the *glaberrima* with improved *sativas* bred for yield potential, where you expect the number of panicles to be high, *glaberrima* compares favorably with improved *sativas*."

These features of *glaberrima* were in line with its reputation for high vegetative growth and high tillerage, says Jones. "But what surprised me was that, contrary to previous belief that *glaberrima* does not respond to improved management, when we planted these *glaberrimas* at low- medium- and high-input levels of management, we found that the number of tillers increased with improved management. So it does respond to improved management. You add fertilizer, you get more panicles. You add herbicides, you get more panicles. That surprised me."

Evaluations for specific stresses also produced unexpected results. In evaluating *glaberrima* for resistance to blast disease an international scoring system developed at IRRI was used. Test scores of 1,3,5,7 and 9 were set, says Jones, with 1 denoting best and 9, terrible. A score of 1 to 3 meant highly resistant, 5 moderately resistant, and 7 to 9 susceptible to highly susceptible to blast. "We found out that *glaberrimas* have very interesting behavior. Some *glaberrimas* are very slow in developing blast. They attain a certain peak, usually 3, maximum 5 resistance level. Then in a few weeks begin to recover." They seemed to be displaying the kind of resistance found in some *sativas*. However, in the *sativas* resistance attains a stage 3 level and stays there, while in *glaberrimas* it attains 3 and recovers to 1." It was the kind of resistance they were looking for to incorporate in WARDA's Wide Crossing program. They seemed to be displaying the kind of resistance found in a few traditional *O. Sativa* (Japonica) like Moroberekan and Lac 23, which have durable resistance to blast.

As a bonus, similar behavior was detected in the tests on iron toxicity, which is regarded as a major problem in West Africa, particularly with lowland rice. Scores would go up to 3 and 5 in the early growth period, but in the fifth or sixth week almost full recovery occurred and at the end of the growth cycle the *glaberrimas* showed only minor symptoms of iron toxicity.

These unforeseen positive traits made the exploitation of *glaberrima* even more desirable. But the tantalizing key question was still whether Jones and his colleagues could find *glaberrima* germplasm with the potential to be crossed successfully with *sativa* to develop a hybridized variety combining the desirable qualities of both species.

Bridging the Gap

A profile of the ideal plant that WARDA wanted was easy to construct. It would combine aspects of the *sativa* structure that make high yields possible with *glaberrima's* amenability to West African conditions. For the sake of suppressing weeds, the plant's architecture would have to resemble the *glaberrima* with its high tillers, luxuriant foliage and droopy lower leaves. The new line should be early maturing and display the tolerance to drought and resistance to blast and other plant diseases and pests of *glaberrima*, but without its tendency to topple and shed grains.

The advantages of crossing *glaberrima* and *sativa* had not gone unrecognized, but *glaberrima* and *sativa* are distinct subtypes and diverge genetically to a degree that inhibits the interchange of genes. This explained the sterility encountered in previous attempts at crossing the two. WARDA's Wide Crossing program made progress, says Jones, because they had come across certain *glaberrimas* with unusual physical characteristics. Two morphological traits distinguish *glaberrima* from *sativa*, lack of secondary branches on the panicle and a much shorter ligule, a structure at the juncture of the stem and leaves. These particular *glaberrimas* had short ligules, but also had panicles with limited secondary branches, says Jones. "They look like *glaberrima*, they do lodge, they have all the traits of *glaberrima* but have maybe 2 or 3 secondary branches just at the base of the panicle, not 4 or 5 like *sativa.* This told me that some form of introgression must have taken place in the wild in these materials. These are the materials we concentrated on in our program with the *sativa.*"

The Wide Crossing program began in late 1991, with standard plant breeding methods employed. Jones says that from his genetics background he knew that it was important to use the plant with the most favorable traits as the senior parent. "We like the *sativa*, it has more advantages than the *glaberrima,* high yield potential, lodging resistance, big panicles. And so we used *sativa* as the female parent and, obviously, the *glabarrima* as the male parent. What we do to the female parent is emasculate the spikelets. Each spikelet is a perfect flower housing the male parts and the female parts.The male part is composed of the anther and the filament. The female part is composed of the stigma and the ovary at the bottom of the spikelet.

"What we do is cut 60% slanting from the tip of the spikelet, clip it off and scoop off all the anthers, or use a vacuum emasculator to suck off all the anthers. We leave in the stigma. To pollinate, we take the pollen grains from the *glaberrima* plant and sprinkle that on the emasculated spikelet of the *sativa*. Then fertilization takes place. This is the process of crossing."

Jones says that after the cross is made, getting seeds from the progeny is not difficult. It is in trying to raise the next generation, known as the F1, that the sterility problem appears. In the first crosses, they got only 1 or 2 percent fertility and saved seed from those plants to raise in the next generation. The key to Wide Crossing's success, according to Jones, was in holding on to the tiny percentage of plants that showed fertility. "We did not throw them away as most people have done in the past. We kept these materials and took them to a second generation."

The next step was to backcross them to the *sativa*. "Why to the *sativa* parent?" asks Jones. "Because we want to retain as many characteristics of the *sativa* as we can. Moreover, what we're looking for is a *sativa* background with some important genes of the *glaberrima* transferred into the *sativa* background. That's why we have to backcross to the *sativa*." After a second backcross, an F2 population was raised in which the percentage of fertility of seed sets mounted to about 30% on average. "At this point, you are talking of true interspecific hybrids," says Jones, "that is plants with genes from two species." However, he says, "You have much variability within that population, variability for blast resistance, variability for growth duration, variability for panicle type, variability for plant type—whether it's spreading like *glaberrima* or erect and compact like *sativa*. Much variability."

True Intermediates

Within this variability, three types of plants can be identified. The first group is made up of plants similar to *sativa* types. Usually their fertility is high, suggesting that little introgression has taken place. The second group is similar to the *glaberrima* parent with perhaps some slight modifications. "These are not of interest," says Jones. "The third type, which we call true intermediates, are probably new types not in any textbook. Basically they are types with a fair proportion of *sativa* and *glaberrima* characteristics. Here fertility will be from zero to about 40 percent or 50 percent in some populations. We make our selection from these—the true intermediates."

In this population you also got what plant breeders refer to as transgressive segregation, where the offspring does better than the best of its parents. In this case, some progeny were taller than the tallest *glaberrima* parent and had larger panicles than the *sativa* and in other ways exhibited hybrid vigor.

But the Wide Crossing enterprise hit a snag. By the time the F4 generation is reached, says Jones, characteristics usually begin to stabilize or "fix." "After that you can say, OK, we've got an advanced line that is fixed within the population for height, panicle type, etc. But in the F4 generation we noticed that the *glaberrima-sativa* progeny populations were still segregating. For some of the materials, although the fertility level increased, it hadn't attained the 90 to 96 percent level you require. The level was still around 60 percent. So this is when we thought that, well, we have to try some other means of fixing these fertility levels. Don't forget that the more generations you go, the higher the likelihood that you'll be losing out something that you have selected.

"That was when we decided to try anther culture to overcome some of the major problems that we encounter with the conventional pedigree method of breeding." Faced with slow fixation, anther culture offered a way to reduce the number of cycles necessary to fix desirable traits. Using progenies from successful crosses, tillers were removed at the flowering stage and taken to the lab. Anthers were then removed from the spikelets and placed in a growth medium. When calli (plant tissue) emerged from the anthers they were transferred to another medium where they developed into small plantlets. These were transferred to a medium with a lower concentration of growth chemicals but with a hardening chemical added to strengthen the plantlets to make it possible to plant them. The use of anther culture speeds up the process so that less than half the seven-year cycle necessary for conventional breeding is required.

If another culture offers such a convenient shortcut in plant breeding, wouldn't it make sense to rely on it rather than the conventional pedigree method? "I don't think the conventional breeding process will go completely," says Jones, "because when we look at the variability within two populations—from anther culture and from conventional breeding—we get more variability from the conventional breeding method. With very careful selection in the conventional method, so that you know which types are good but for which the sterility is high, you can then pass them through anther culture. I believe that the two complement each other."

With experience, confidence has grown. "Now if it is difficult in F1 we are not discouraged. We take it to the F2 or F3 or F4. So long as we've got one or two populations with 5% fertility we can select from, we feel that at some stage in the process we are going to add this anther culture process and we're going to get some fixed lines," says Jones. "So we are not letting up at the F1 or F2 stage. It's time consuming, but it's worth doing because eventually we are going to get an interspecific hybrid that will combine important traits between *glaberrima* and *sativa*."

A False Alarm

Jones concedes that there have been moments of uncertainty or worse. A plant breeding hazard is that even after a new plant line seems to be fixed, some form of what is termed instability may appear. In early 1996, Wide Crossing materials had been planted in hydromorphic and irrigated conditions in Côte d'Ivoire. Jones says that a week or two later, "we went to the field and saw these white seedlings, probably 20 percent white seedlings among the green seedlings. I was worried. That could mean some form of mutation taking place." Two weeks after that Jones went back and the white coloration had disappeared. "I marked these plants and some gave very high yields. Then we planted them again in the rainy season. Again, in at least one or two we found the same behavior, but at very reduced level.

"Now they are all green again. You won't find any white plants. This is maybe a sign of instability in one or two populations but this occurred in less than 5 percent. There were no other serious signs of instability—like sterility. If we got that it would be serious. If you got 10 percent sterility that would be very worrying."

Use of anther culture started in late 1993. By proceeding on parallel tracks, the Wide Crossing project in 1995 got its first fixed lines. These were evaluated the next year. Jones said that WARDA's continuum program leader Michael Dingkuhn oversaw trials of these materials using various levels of nitrogen fertilizer. At 80 kilograms of fertilizer per hectare in small upland plots he got a yield of 5.9 tonnes per hectare from one of the progenies and more than 4 t/ha for most of the others. At zero level input, the yield was 3.8 t/ha The last is double to triple the typical yield of a subsistence farmer growing rice in upland conditions.

Jones got lower yields in his own trials, but this was not unexpected since the other trials were conducted in virgin uplands, which denotes land cultivated the first year after a long fallow period. Jones's trial was in fields that had been cultivated for 3 years after a short, 3-year fallow period. "I raised a crop for the 4th year so it was really an exhausted plot," he says. "I evaluated material at low input and high input, not zero level. Low input in this case means felling of big trees, application of 20 kg of nitrogen fertilizer per hectare and carrying out weeding, keeping plots clean. We got up to 3 t/ha at low input and up to 4 to 5 t/ha at high input levels." These too, were very encouraging results.

Jones and his colleagues see the potential for using these fixed lines in other than upland conditions. In 1995, trials were conducted with shallow and deepwater rice with what are described as very good results. "We think there is potential for extending these materials to other rainfed production systems," says Jones. Yields may not be very high, but they can still be used in breeding programs for typical lowland types."

Looking back, Jones is forthright about the key to success so far. "We stumbled into groups of materials in which some form of introgression had taken place in the past. They showed some compatibility with *sativas* and from there we have expanded the base because we are using these as bridging materials to cross other *glaberrimas* and *sativas*. So we bridged the gap."

Touch of a Plant Breeder

The Wide Crossing program was a complicated affair and required careful planning. Accurate records are obviously critical and WARDA researchers have adapted a package of plant breeding software for the program so that all record keeping is computerized. And biotechnology is obviously playing an increasing part in the development of new plant varieties.

That does not mean that Jones can sit in his office and rely on technology to do the fieldwork. The key act of selecting which plants will go to the next generation requires a plant breeder's presence in the field or screen house and the job retains elements of an art as well as a science. Some would suggest that plant breeders are born not just made.

Jones says that until be got a job at Rokupr in Sierra Leone after finishing his undergraduate degree, "I had been thinking I would be a soil scientist. When I went for the interview, they said you did so well in breeding in your undergraduate work why not concentrate as a breeder. They pushed it to me. I just became a breeder. And I really loved it.

"I have the touch of a breeder. I see things that other people cannot see. What plants are good. You can believe me when I say I talk to my plants, say 'you've got that, the others have not got that. So why not see what we get out of this.' That worked well for mangrove swamp rice, it worked well when I went to Cameroon," says Jones.

"When it comes to selection in the field I am there. I never leave selection to even my immediate assistants. Everybody is involved. We all like working together. My assistant or the observateur will call and say, 'Dr. Jones, come and take a look at this plant.' What we do is move along the rows and look at each population. I take one population. Somebody else takes one population. If you find something that is very good you get the others to come and see. And so we can say with that and with that I think we've made progress."

Jones says that his assistants love the work and excel at it but this was not true when he arrived. "I must tell you that we had problems initially. We had guys who had been in the system, but the way that they were handling selection from the segregated populations, it was terrible. We had to build the team right from scratch. How to do selection. What you look for when you are selecting. And not everybody can do selection. When you visit the field three times in the day, you see a certain amount of good material in the first visit. When you come for the second visit when it's hot, the leaves may fold, the plants may not look happy. You say this is because the humidity was high in the morning it looked nice. But look at the way this material is now.

"You have to be gifted to be able to select from within 200 plants one or two or three that will make it as a variety. Breeders are different from the plant pathologists. The pathologist will go to the field and he will say, 'Look, blast resistant,' and he will select that material. The breeder will go and say it's not just blast resistance. What about yield? What about the farmer's request for varieties with intermediate panicles? What about panicle exsercion? Sometimes the panicle is wrapped in a sheath. If it comes out of the sheath you have complete panicle exsercion. If it is not fully exserted they have to remove the sheath to have it, and farmers do not go for those materials.

"Sometimes a pathologist will say, 'I nominated that variety. You have not used it again.' I will say no, we used it in one cross. We've got progeny from that cross and we are now using them in other crosses, because we do realize that, as far as blast is concerned, it's a good material, but, as far as other traits are concerned that is not a good material. So we used it to mix that particular trait for which it's good (into) a more suitable variety of material that we're now using in other crosses," says Jones. "So the breeder will look at these things, take the general view into consideration as against the special area scientist."

A Broader Strategy

Despite the encouraging results of field trials, it was clear that WARDA was a long way from fully exploiting the Wide Crossing work. In December of 1996, Japan and the United States joined with UNDP in sponsoring a meeting in Côte d'Ivoire to formulate a broader strategy on the interspecific hybridization of rice in Africa and beyond.

Participants at a scientific workshop at M'be, including leading rice geneticists, found that the WARDA materials offered the potential for substantial increases in productivity of rice farmers in the region and compiled a list of research priorities to realize that potential. With this positive technical assessment in hand, representatives from Japan the United States, UNDP and other interested parties held planning sessions in Abidjan. The result was agreement on launching of a project under the aegis of UNDP in collaboration with three CGIAR centers, IRRI, CIAT and WARDA, with WARDA as lead center and project coordinator. The project would run for 3 years at a cost of $1.75 million with funding provided by Japan, the United States and UNDP. The aim would be not only to create new rice varieties, but also to ensure that poor farmers would be able to use them.

Irrigated Rice

Rice has been grown in West Africa for many centuries, but cultivation of rice under irrigation began on a large-scale way there only after World War I. The French were the initiators with a major project known as the Office du Niger in the so-called inland delta of the Niger River in what is now Mali. This set a pattern of government investment and control, including forced labor in the case of the Office, that dominated irrigated rice projects in the region for the rest of the century. Most such ventures were attempted along major rivers, particularly the Niger and Senegal in the Sahel. Rainfed rice dominated in wetter regions to the south.

In francophone countries, demand for rice had been stimulated through a trading and marketing system based on a sort of triangular trade that was most highly developed in Senegal. Colonial authorities there encouraged cultivation of groundnuts as a cash crop to produce oil for export to France. To replace the millet and sorghum that farmers had formerly grown for food, rice was imported from French colonies in Indo China and sold cheaply.

After World War II, domestic production of rice was promoted to reduce reliance on imported rice. Big irrigated perimeters were developed on the lower Senegal River and a large number of peasant families settled there. The farmers' unfamiliarity with rice cultivation combined with organizational and agronomic problems to produce disappointing results.

Following independence in 1960, the new government of Senegal continued to rely heavily on groundnut exports, but experienced an economic squeeze as France ended a subsidy for groundnuts and the cost of rice rose on the world market. The effects of the Sahel drought and the oil embargo of the early 1970s increased the government's zeal to exploit the agricultural potential of the Senegal River. Senegal joined with Mauritania and Mali as partners in a dam construction project to develop the Senegal River valley, to be mainly financed by a group of Arab oil states and European development organizations. Despite questions about debt repayment and doubts about the environmental, health and social effects of the project, a salt intrusion dam in the delta and a high dam on a main tributary of the Senegal were completed in the last half of the 1980s.

Senegal hoped to produce a rice surplus that would make possible cuts in rice imports. Responsibility was given to a regional development agency, the *Société nationale d'amenagement et d'exploitation du delta du fleuve Sénégal et des vallées du fleuve Sénégal et de la Falémé* (SAED). SAED was to undertake land preparation, provide farmers with seed and fertilizer, and specify what crops would be grown. The government set the price at which rice was to be sold.

The plan came into conflict with alternative schemes organized in the lower and middle Senegal valley by peasant farmers. They formed *groupements villageois* and cultivated small perimeters irrigated with water drawn from the river by diesel pumps mounted on floats that allowed them to adjust to the rise and fall of the river. Tensions between the government program and the village enterprises was described by anthropologist Adrian Adams as a conflict between *developpement functionnair* and *developpement paysanne*. The village groups received support from private voluntary agencies and bilateral aid agencies. As the 1980s progressed and economic reforms took hold, the government cut back its intervention in agriculture and moved to liberalize markets, abating tensions somewhat. Senegal's experience was roughly similar to that of other West African countries with such irrigated rice projects.

A Strategy for the Sahel

Even before WARDA's move to Côte d'Ivoire, a decision had been made to continue a significant research program on irrigated rice. Terry recalls, however, that when the old WARDA's Sahel operation came under scrutiny there appeared to be no coherent overall strategy. At one time, WARDA's Sahel program mustered a dozen or more professionals and served as Senegal's de facto research program on irrigated rice. By the late 1980s, the staff had been reduced to a few professionals. Under the new WARDA regime, all professional positions had been declared open for international competition. A clean sweep of incumbents in the Sahel program followed. Kwame Miezan, a rice breeder who had headed WARDA's upland rice program in Bouaké for the old WARDA, was named to head the new Sahel team.

The Sahel program at the time occupied office and laboratory space and carried out research in fields provided by Senegal's institute for agricultural research (ISRA). The arrangements were less than ideal. The WARDA offices were in the region's principal city, St. Louis, at the mouth of the Senegal river, the labs were at Richard Toll more than 100 km upriver and field experiments were conducted at Fanaye another 70 km along the river. The practical result was that WARDA scientists spent a disproportionate amount of time at desks in St. Louis and on the road connecting St. Louis, Richard Toll and Fanaye rather than in labs or fields. In addition, WARDA-ISRA attempts to operate joint research programs had come to little.

It happened that about the time Miezan took over his new assignment, ISRA gave WARDA notice to vacate space to make room for a research team beginning a new project. With Terry's backing, Miezan negotiated a connection with SAED, the regional parastatal. The connection was attractive to WARDA because SAED offered immediate access to farmers. By coincidence, SAED was downsizing as a result of the government push to privatize and was able to offer the facilities that the WARDA Sahel program now occupies at N'diaye about 25 km upriver from St. Louis. WARDA took over and converted two villas at the SAED establishment there and by 1991 had offices, labs and modest conference facilities as well as experimental fields all in one place. The Fanaye site was further developed to allow research in the conditions that prevail in the middle valley of the Senegal.

Double Cropping the Aim

WARDA planners devising a new strategy for the Sahel had to address a major challenge. To justify the investment in irrigation, farmers would have to produce two rice crops a year rather than one. Most farmers raised a single rice crop during the rainy season that runs from June to October. In the succeeding cool dry season from November to March, many grew other cereals or vegetables on the same plots.

A shift to double cropping of rice would not be easy. The Sahel is synonymous with periodic severe drought, but even in the best of times each season has its tribulations for farmers. Extremes in temperature, wind-borne dust driven in from the desert, and soil salinity and alkalinity are constants in the Sahel. The assaults of weeds, plant diseases, insects, and marauding birds must be factored in. And the inexperience of farmers with rice cultivation multiplies the difficulties.

WARDA's response was to broaden its research to achieve a better understanding of the Sahel environment. The rationale was that such knowledge would guide development of germplasm suited to conditions in the Sahel and, thereby, reduce the risks for farmers. Peter Matlon recalls that most of the plant varieties grown by rice farmers under irrigated conditions in Senegal at the time were introduced by the old WARDA from imported varieties in the 1970s. But results of yield trials of new materials to replace these varieties proved frustratingly inconsistent from year to year, making it hard to achieve real progress in rice breeding for the region.

The hypothesis was that temperature fluctuations were mainly to blame for the variations in yield. If temperatures fall below 16 degrees centigrade when rice panicles are forming—known as the booting stage—what is called cold sterility results. Extreme cold turns rice grains into white powder. Above the 35 degree mark, heat induced sterility occurs. A systematic study of temperature patterns and their effects on different rice varieties was given priority. Accordingly, an early appointment to the reformed Sahel program was plant physiologist Michael Dingkuhn. It was Dingkuhn who led the effort to diagnose the problem of variable performance and develop a practical "cropping calendar" for farmers.

Information was gathered from local weather records to establish when temperature highs and lows occurred. It was also important to gain more reliable knowledge of what is termed crop duration, that is the time from planting to harvest for specific crop varieties. Dingkuhn's solution was to work with researchers in Senegal, Mali and Burkina Faso in creating "rice gardens." Small plots of rice were planted at two-week intervals over several years and careful records kept on growing conditions and stages of plant development for different varieties.

Using data from these trials, Dingkuhn developed a computer model dubbed RIDEV (for rice development) that incorporates a range of data on sites, plant varieties and management options. Planting dates for specific varieties were identified to help farmers avoid temperature highs and lows at crucial points in the growth cycle. Peasant rice farmers in West Africa are unlikely to have access to computers, but WARDA has made the computer model available to NARS, farmers associations and NGOs and provided training in its use. For more direct communication, WARDA tried putting RIDEV recommendations in table form and posting them at farmers' meetings. The response indicated that the tables would be used.

A follow-on project complementary to RIDEV was launched in 1996. It is aimed at examining farmers' problems with yield and productivity and identifying ways to reduce their impact. The research design by Marco Wopereis, the Sahel station agronomist, and Cynthia Donovan, a production economist and Rockefeller postdoctoral fellow, emphasizes contact with farmers and also involves farm organizations and extension workers as well as researchers in

Burkina Faso, Mali and Senegal. A combination of on farm trials and surveys will be used with the idea of developing a methodology that can be more widely applied.

WARDA is also branching out in an effort to respond to consequences of privatization. For example, WARDA\Sahel is backing development of a small-scale rice thresher\cleaner combination. WARDA teamed with IRRI in the Philippines and SAED and ISRA in Senegal and worked with a local artisan to produce a prototype based on an IRRI design. An agricultural machinery manufacturer agreed to produce a small number of the machines. Early tests by farmers and financial analyses were promising, but whether the machine will find buyers depends not only on its merits but on the market that has emerged with economic liberalization. In the past, it was the government and donors that bore the costs and took the gamble on investment in new technology. Because of the economic reforms, it is increasingly up to the private sector, which is often unwilling or unable to assume the risks.

For rice growers in the Sahelian countries—and for WARDA—this entrepreneurial weakness is probably most serious in respect to limitations on seed production and distribution. This restricts the availability of new WARDA varieties. Certainly, the consequences of economic reforms complicates the task for WARDA, which must not only create useful new technology, but address the question of how to get it into the hands of the people for whom it is designed and convince them to use it.

Natural Resource Management

With both rainfed and irrigated rice, WARDA research has a dual objective: increasing the yields of rice plants, but doing so in ways that are sustainable, that is, do not degrade the natural resource base for the future. From the start, the CGIAR centers recognized the importance of the interactions between agriculture and ecosystems. Natural resources research is seen as the key to understanding those interactions and achieving sustainability.

Plant breeders have played a conspicuous role in the green revolution, but modern agricultural research and particularly natural resources research is a team enterprise drawing in scientists from an array of disciplines including agronomists, plant pathologists and physiologists, entomologists, soil scientists and hydrologists as well as social and behavioral scientists—economists, sociologists and anthropologists. As the CGIAR's emphasis on sustainability has grown, natural resources management research, as it is styled, has acquired a larger place in programs and budgets and the stress on multidisciplinary research has increased.

For WARDA, the fragility of West African ecosystems, makes natural resources research particularly important and challenging. Representative of such research at WARDA was a study in the mid 1990s on salinization in the Senegal River delta. Farmers in cooperatives in the delta were giving up on double cropping of irrigated rice in large part because of rising levels of salinity in the soil in their fields. The rice plant can be bred to tolerate salinity relatively well, but irrigated rice projects in the Senegal River valley have a history of succumbing after a few years to plummeting yields and of fields being abandoned due in large part to salinization. Salt buildup has two main causes. Salts are either brought to the surface from ground water through capillary action or are deposited by irrigation water that is brought in. Groundwater in the delta tends to be saline and the water-table level quite high, which intensifies the salinization problem.

In their surveys, WARDA researchers looked hard at field topography, soil characteristics, water management and cropping systems. As might be expected, damage was less serious where what is regarded as basic good irrigation practice was followed. That is, where there was proper grading, good drainage and adequate and timely flushing of fields to remove salts. Soils in low areas were found to be much more saline than in higher parts because of pooling and subsequent evaporation of water. Fields at the end of the irrigation line had high salinity because of the condition of the water when it reached them.

The implications of the research are clear enough. Prevention of rapid deterioration of irrigation projects in the Sahel requires the right sort of land preparation, choice of soils and water management. But no simple formula suffices. Conditions in individual projects vary and many factors have to be taken into account. For example, researchers argue that it is desirable that water table levels be monitored and, if necessary, controlled, perhaps by planting trees whose root systems will tap into groundwater and reduce its levels, and that drainage water be disposed of without creating problems elsewhere.

Protecting the Ecosystem

The CGIAR is being pushed by concerns about the environment and loss of biodiversity and an awareness that it could find itself offering new high yielding crop varieties that farmers could not use because of natural resource factors. The group is, therefore, anxious to insure that new technologies not harm the ecosystems where they are introduced.

For an adequate analysis of a proposed irrigation project it is necessary to take a broad look at the relevant physical and social factors as a system. A systems approach is now being strongly embraced by the group. What is envisioned is research that includes not only agriculture, but livestock raising, forestry, fisheries, and other activities that impact the ecosystem. The CGIAR label applied to the effort is integrated resource management research.

The key word is management. And the CGIAR's aim to learn enough about natural resources to manage them in the cause of agricultural sustainability is an ambitious one. Achieving a comprehensive understanding of an ecosystem and providing viable solutions that are useful to poor farmers are formidable tasks. In some spheres the methodologies are simply not adequate. And integration of the results of research requires a degree of interdisciplinary collaboration that is still not easily attained. In addition, in many parts of the region, institutions capable of coordinating integrated resource management do not exist.

The expansion of the CGIAR in the early 1990s to include centers devoted to research on forestry, aquatic resources, and irrigation management offers greater opportunities for collaboration in research. And the group's improved ability to measure sustainability and undertake joint efforts with NARS also increases its leverage on natural resource management. But even the best intentions may not be enough if current research methods must be relied on.

Biotechnology

World population is expected to double in little more than a generation, with the growth coming disproportionately in developing countries. WARDA has made solid progress with its research on both the continuum and irrigated rice programs but, even by the most optimistic estimates, the current state of the art in agricultural research will not make possible increases in crop yields sufficient to meet future food needs in West Africa. Biotechnology offers a promising route to increasing food production, but along with its unexampled potential biotechnology poses an unprecedented set of challenges for the CGIAR.

The term biotechnology connotes a broad range of scientific techniques and tools, including tissue culture procedures used in the WARDA's Wide Crossing program. However, greater advances in productivity in agriculture are anticipated from what is termed bioengineering. This involves the insertion of genes into food crops to make them more resistant to diseases and pests or more tolerant of drought and other extreme conditions. The transfer of genes not only from the same species but from unrelated plant species or animals permits development of so-called transgenic plants capable of passing on these genetic modifications to their progeny.

Promise and Problems

The implications of bioengineering ignited controversy on grounds of safety, ethics and economics. Although philosophical questions abound in the debate, the objections cluster mainly about issues of safety and access. In respect to safety, critics raise questions about unintended consequences, for example, the chance that transfer of genes into food crops could trigger allergies in humans that consume them or might kill beneficial as well as harmful bacteria. Also raising worries is the possibility of the accidental escape of genes from transgenic plants. For example, injected genes that give food plants resistance to insects might be transferred to weeds via an escape of pollen, creating superweeds. Known as the gene flow problem, this sort of "outcrossing" is seen as particularly threatening to poor farmers in developing countries.

On the matter of access, a main concern is that poor people in developing countries that are the main source of crop germplasm will not be able to afford high yielding crop varieties based on genetic materials originating in their countries but developed by biotechnology companies or agribusinesses in developed countries.

A maze of patent law and international agreements has been constructed under the rubric of so-called plant-breeders rights. Proponents argue that protection in the market is necessary to encourage private enterprise to make the investment required to develop better crop varieties through new technology. A key dispute is over patenting of life forms, in this case plant genes. Critics object that granting control over both products and processes not only confers monopoly power but can deter further innovation.

Since the debate over biotechnology began in earnest in the middle 1970s, the CGIAR position has been to maximize the free use of genetic materials for crop development and, where possible, to advance the interests of poor farmers in developing countries. The CGIAR has found it difficult to play an active part in this fast moving field. In the technical realm, the group has not found it easy to decide where it should operate on the biotechnology spectrum. Should the centers expand their research in biotechnology? Or should they act as agents, relaying technology from institutions doing advanced research in the sector and providing training in biotechnology to scientists in developing countries? The uncertainty is compounded in the dimension of policy because the CGIAR, by design, has avoided such highly charged political issues and has lacked the expertise to deal with complex intellectual property questions.

Bioegineering initiatives, however, have moved beyond the theoretical and even the experimental stages. The CGIAR is, therefore, under pressure to define its position more fully. The issues are not the sort that can be addressed by the individual centers on a case-by-case basis and policy will have to made for the CGIAR as a whole. The CGIAR's bonds with both developed and developing countries could enable it to play a mediating role in the intensifying controversy, although by doing so the group might put its apolitical status in jeopardy. Biotechnology is a tough but unavoidable subject in the discussion of system-wide change launched by the CGIAR in 1997. The issues they address are controversial; certainly they are crucial to the CGIAR's future.

Monty Jones

Monty Jones's background and a personality that combines confidence with a modest demeanor make him seem a natural for his role in the Wide Crossing project. He was born in the rice growing country of Sierra Leone, but spent most of his early life in the capital, Freetown. It was only after he finished high school there and got a job on a rice project at a small experiment station outside Freetown that he says he "got to know agriculture and decided I wanted to be an agriculturist."

He earned a bachelor's degree in agriculture at Sierra Leone's N'jala College in 1974 and then, after working for a year as a teacher in Freetown, went to Sierra Leone's rice research station at Rokupr as a research assistant. A few months later he was awarded a fellowship to IRRI in the Philippines and spent 14 months there, the first six months in general training in rice production and the next eight attached to the rice-breeding department. At the time, the department was headed by an American rice breeder, W. Ronnie Coffman, who, coincidentally, was later to play a prominent supporting role in the transformation of WARDA.

Jones returned to Rokupr and for several years gravitated between Rokupr and Birmingham University in Britain where he did graduate work. He carried out his thesis research in Sierra Leone and received his D.Phil. in 1983. For the next five years he continued at Rokupr as a member of the national staff, but worked on a WARDA mangrove swamp rice program, eventually taking charge of its breeding activities.

He says that this period helped him establish himself as a plant breeder. Although WARDA was not involved in technology development at the time, he says that as a national staff member "I was able to carry out hybridization work. So today, most of the rice varieties cultivated in mangrove swamps in West Africa, in the six countries that raise mangrove rice (Gambia, Guinea, Guinea Bissau, Nigeria, Senegal, Sierra Leone) either I developed or we popularized,"

Jones then spent two-and-a-half years in Cameroon working on a project of the CGIAR's International Institute of Tropical Agriculture. "Cameroon had a rice program 10 years before I went there, but not a breeding program," said Jones. "Cameroon is unique from the rest of West Africa," said Jones. "They have upland conditions, irrigated conditions not found in most of the region, high altitude, low temperature, similar to what you find in Rwanda."

"All the varieties coming out of previous breeding programs from Africa and Asia somehow did not thrive at low temperatures—low temperatures combined with African problems— blast disease, etc. There was a need to attack those problems, so we started a breeding program there. Quite a number of very good varieties are now grown in Cameroon and areas with similar conditions, like Rwanda.

"In Cameroon, compared to countries like Sierra Leone and Guinea Bissau, rice was, comparatively, a new crop, grown for about 20 years. A majority of the area under rice is irrigated, with very good water control. It's in the extreme north of the country. They used to get the best yields in the region, about 7 tonnes a hectare. Upland rice yields only about 2 tonnes a hectare.

"The government raised seedlings in its own nurseries, distributed seedlings to farmers, helped the farmers to plant them, supplied the fertilizer. But the financial future was not good. They had the director of this, the director of that. The cost of production went up too high. Most of it went to finance fat, all those directors. Imported rice was much cheaper than rice produced domestically. This resulted in serious problems. They had to dismantle all these very big irrigated development projects, allow the farmers to do their own thing."

In 1991, Jones left Cameroon and joined WARDA as upland rice breeder. His responsibilities were later enlarged to put him in charge of WARDA's rice hybridization effort, not just for upland rice, but for the entire continuum.

WARDA plant breeder Monty Jones, leader of Wide Crossing\NERICA program.

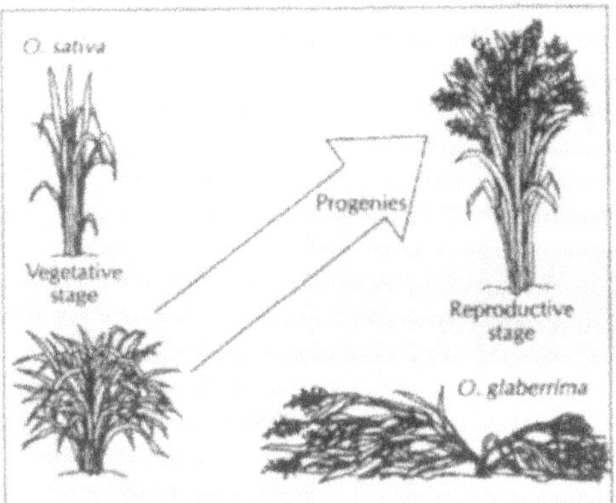

Drawing illustrates aim of Wide Crossing program to capture weed-competitive traits of *O. glaberrima* during the vegetative state and the agronomically valuable traits of *O. sativa* during the reproductive period.

O. sativa

O. glaberrima

Experiment plot at WARDA's field station at N´diaye, Senegal. Station buildings are in background. Box on post is micro-meteorological recording device.

A stripper-harvester designed by IRRI in Philippines is tested in Senegal delta.

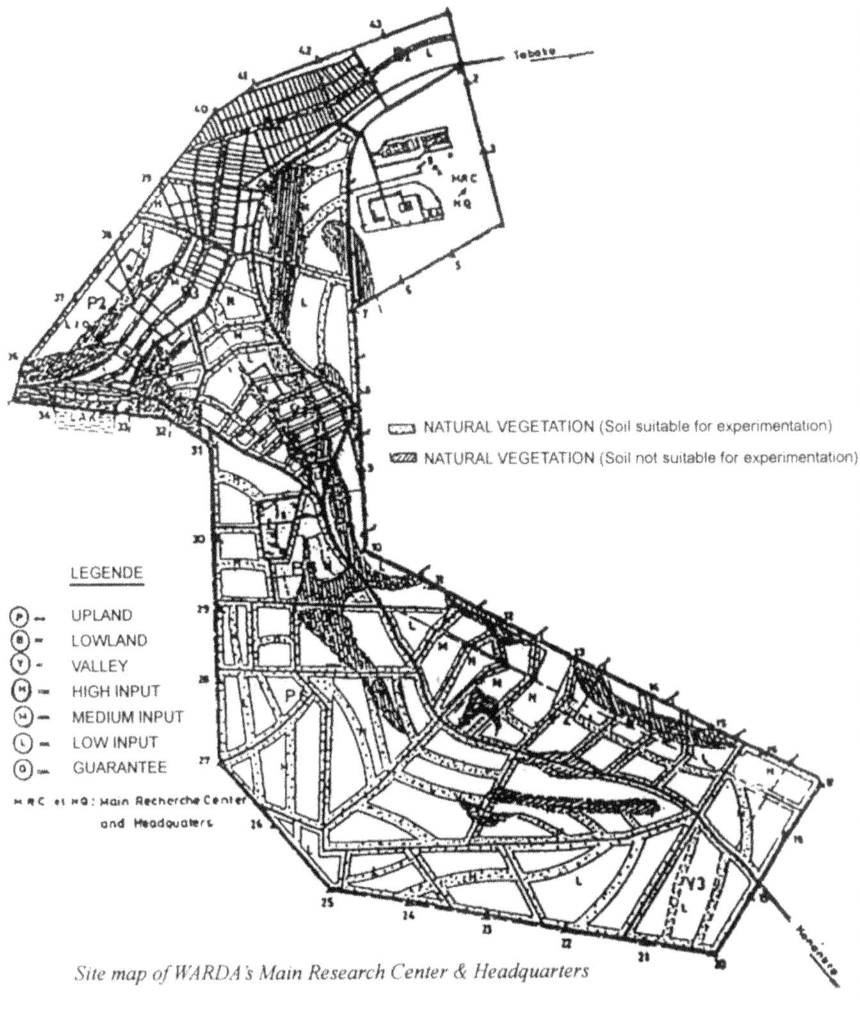

Site map of WARDA's Main Research Center & Headquarters

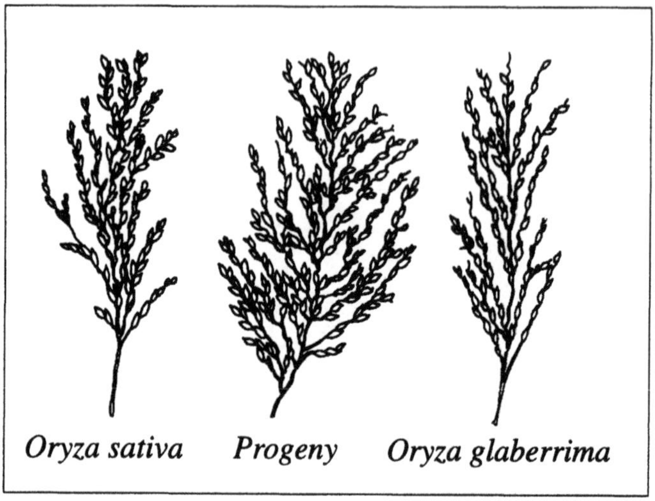

Drawing illustrates structure of *sativa* and *glaberrima* parents and progeny.

This field experiment is designed to test drought tolerance in rice varieties.

4 Redefining Partnership

Devolution the Goal

A major assumption of the founders of the CGIAR in the 1970s was that the organization would deal with a crisis in Third World food production and work itself out of existence by fostering the capacity for agricultural research in developing countries. In recent years, CGIAR donors have begun to complain that they have given substantial amounts of money over a long period to the international centers to improve national programs and now want more evidence that the investment has been worthwhile.

"Devolution" has been the term used to describe the process of handing off responsibilities to national scientists. Although no timetable has ever been put forward, the CGIAR has structured its research with devolution in mind. The group operates across a spectrum of strategic, applied and adaptive research. In CGIAR parlance, strategic research is at the "upstream" end, adaptive research at the "downstream" end of the spectrum. The premise has been that as national programs grew stronger they would progressively take over downstream research. Upstream activities would remain largely the province of the international centers, at least for the foreseeable future.

Upstream or strategic research is usually defined as having international relevance. Prime examples are the collection and conservation of plant germplasm. The CGIAR centers' genebanks are among the most important repositories of plant germplasm in the world and serve as a bulwark of biodiversity. With their scientific expertise, the centers are uniquely fitted to use this wealth of germplasm to do what is called pre-breeding work, for instance, enhancing germplasm by the introgression of genes from wild relatives and other unrelated species through biotechnology.

As the international centers move upstream, the scenario calls for the national programs to assume responsibility for adapting improved crops to particular ecologies and for many aspects of research on production systems. This is already occurring in Asia where several countries have capable national agricultural research systems (NARS). India, for example, has some 22,000 scientists in its national program. Increasingly, the stronger NARS are asserting their ability to take over more sophisticated sorts of research from

CGIAR centers and expressing annoyance at the slow pace of change.

In sub-Saharan Africa, on the other hand, most NARS are severely underfunded and in some cases still short of competent scientists. What appears to be indicated is a CGIAR strategy that can be implemented variably according to the capabilities of its partners. Logical though this may be, it spells a complicated transition for the CGIAR. A priority for WARDA and other CGIAR centers operating in sub-Saharan Africa is to provide support for NARS in the form of training for individual national scientists and help with institution building. WARDA has proved itself better than most international centers at doing just that.

Networks to Task Forces

For WARDA, developing a promising new plant variety is only half the battle. Adapting it for specific environments in West Africa and persuading farmers to adopt it cannot be done by WARDA alone. Necessary players in the process are the NARS whose scientists and extension workers provide the main connection to the farmers. Unfortunately, the NARS in many WARDA member countries have not been up to the job. Most agricultural research and extension services inherited by West African countries at independence had few trained African staff, became politicized and suffered from a chronic lack of funds. Donors recognized the problem and in the 1980s gave substantial support to African NARS. However, West African governments were struggling with structural adjustment regimes and invested little of their own funds in agricultural research. The NARS relied heavily on donor financing to operate; when these funds declined, the NARS were further weakened.

WARDA's ability to disseminate new technologies on its own is decidedly limited. WARDA and other CGIAR centers are research organizations and lack the resources and personnel to perform the outreach activities required. In fact, such efforts are sharply circumscribed by the CGIAR mandate. The rules deter centers from taking initiatives that might offend territorial sensitivities of national scientists. On the other hand, the restrictions do offer a degree of protection in cases where host countries try to inveigle CGIAR centers into filling the gaps in their own programs.

Despite the obstacles, the CGIAR centers from the start have considered it essential to work with scientists in national systems and set out to do so by organizing networks designed to link the scientists to the center and to each other. The typical network focused on a particular crop or agricultural problem.

Terry and Matlon agreed on the potential of networks but saw serious shortcomings in the prevailing model. Both of them had direct experience of working with West African NARS and networks. Terry had been director of international programs at IITA and involved in the development of IITA's root crop network. Matlon helped organize ICRISAT's regional sorghum network.

Asked what lessons he had learned at IITA that carried over when he moved to WARDA, Terry says, "We were so arrogant. We were the ones working in the international centers. We knew the science. We knew the directions in which to go. People in national programs were just recipients. I found out that we ran into a lot of problems because there was resentment, jealousy, feelings of non-cooperation. IITA people came back to the center saying 'What do these guys want? We're providing technology for them.' Well, what they wanted, pure and simple, was not to be recipients, they wanted to be partners. So I learned that if you're going to have a really solid joint program, you have to find out how you can make them partners."

The main limitation WARDA's leaders saw in the typical network in West Africa was in their being designed mainly to disseminate information and CGIAR technology. Networks operated in a top-down fashion with the international centers calling the tune. What Terry and Matlon had in mind was a network with a genuine research function in which national scientists participated in a much more active way.

The WARDA Formula

The genesis of the revised networks can be traced to WARDA's annual rice review held in 1988 in Bouaké. This event, sponsored by WARDA, had been an annual congregation of rice scientists from the region to discuss progress and priorities. Terry and Matlon felt that it had become more social occasion than scientific meeting and did not justify the considerable expense. In their view, such a forum could never serve as a mechanism for real cooperation. The next year, with the model of the think tank in mind, two working groups were formed, one on crop improvement, the other on resource management. These working groups were asked what was being done wrong at WARDA and at other international centers in efforts to promote cooperation and, also, what sort of mechanisms would help to build healthier partnerships. Out of these discussions came the WARDA task forces, a name given the redesigned networks to imply that something would be produced.

The working groups met five times between 1989 and 1993, designating different task forces and setting a timetable for launching them. By 1993, about half the planned task forces had been organized and the working groups terminated their own existence. In 1996, nine task forces were operating, each bringing together scientists from the region who were working on the same problems in rice research—upland rice breeding, lowland rainfed rice breeding, mangrove swamp rice breeding, irrigated rice breeding, problem soils, rice based cropping systems, rice economics, integrated pest management and Sahel resource management.

Matlon concedes that WARDA generated the idea for the task forces, but insists that their design was the joint product of national scientists and their WARDA counterparts. He says that the main reason for the success of the task forces is that national scientists "really feel that they conceived and designed the mechanism. There's a great deal of loyalty to it."

The task forces embodied several new concepts. First, there was a strong consensus to move away from the prevailing top-down style of priority setting and management of networks. Another important departure from past patterns was acknowledgement of differences in quality among the NARS in the region. West African NARS vary greatly in size and competence, depending mainly on the size and wealth of their countries. NARS in small countries have usually tried to cover the full range of research activities, but lacked the capacity to do so satisfactorily. At least half of WARDA's member countries fall into this category. Networks in sub-Sahara Africa typically ignored the differences and operated on what amounted to a one-size-fits-all philosophy in respect to NARS.

WARDA task forces were designed to follow the principle of comparative advantage, allocating research tasks according to the capabilities of NARS and of individual scientists. In perhaps the most significant shift, national scientists take responsibility for particular aspects of research projects and are assisted by modest financial support to carry out the work. NARS now frequently agree to take the lead in research tasks in which they have particular strength and which can benefit the entire region. These arrangements have enhanced the spirit of cooperation and contributed to building research capacity in West Africa.

Individual task forces were to be run by steering committees made up of national scientists. Matlon says that over the years each task force shaped its operations in its own way, but that there is plenty of cross-fertilization of ideas among the task forces. One group may try something new in terms of how decisions are made or the way monitoring tours are organized. "If it worked," says Matlon, "others would say, 'This looks good, let's try it.'"

New Leverage

An example of the leverage the task forces can exert is the upland breeding task force's instigation of significant changes in the manner new breeding materials are distributed to NARS for testing and adaptation. During the 1980s, the International Network for the Genetic Evaluation of Rice (INGER) managed by IRRI was the dominant source of rice germplasm for national programs in West Africa. The network provided a wide range of genetic material and information on how a specific material was likely to perform.

INGER's practice was to offer collections of packages of seeds focused on particular plant types or stresses. The problem with these so-called "fixed nurseries" was that each nursery contained the same varieties and was sent to West African countries on what amounted to a take-it-or-leave-it basis. WARDA began making germplasm available on similar terms. Weak national programs, in particular, had difficulty sorting out what was useful to them.

WARDA's upland rice task force wanted a scheme that would be much more responsive to the needs of particular national programs, says Matlon. "A country might specify, 'Our priority is not drought, it's weeds.' or ' what we want are materials that are slightly different, longer duration, a different grain type.' So you end up with 20 or more slightly different nurseries." The old system might have made sense 20 years ago because many breeders really did not know their own environments and could not diagnose their problems very well, says Matlon. "That's no longer the case. You're insulting a NARS breeder if you're assuming that you can make the selection, that you can send out 130 lines and he should somehow rummage through them and screen out the two or three that fit him well. He knows his environment, he's sufficiently well trained and has the confidence to say 'I don't need your 130, what I need are 12 which fit this profile. Send them to me.'" NARS can now ask for the materials they want, specifying plant characteristics. And a catalogue is being produced to make the process easier.

In addition to requesting a more flexible scheme, the task force asked that INGER and WARDA create a single mechanism to avoid duplication and cut down on overload. WARDA and IRRI accordingly agreed to join forces to provide nurseries and to base a coordinator at WARDA. For West Africa, what is unusual is not so much that INGER was reformed, but that the push came from scientists in the national programs. Not incidentally, WARDA's formula for partnership was one of the strong factors in its favor when WARDA was under scrutiny in the 1993 system-wide rice review.

An Open Center

With its task forces, WARDA made partnership more than a platitude and managed to serve its own interests as well. In another aspect of its operations WARDA has also given partnership a new twist and, in the process, found an additional way to transcend the limitations on its own staff and budget. Facing up to funding realities, WARDA strategists developed their own concept of an open center. Matlon recalls that "At least as early as '91 it became clear that our core support was unlikely to grow to the level necessary, in the foreseeable future, to bring on board all of the disciplines that we had originally anticipated in our medium term plan. So we began to look at how we might be able to do two things. One, get people in key disciplines that we were not able to support with core resources. Two, create linkages to northern institutions so we could benefit from their technical backstopping and establish collaborative relationships." He acknowledges a third consideration. "We also saw this as a way of increasing our funding. Because more and more, donors were moving towards a formula which ties their assistance to collaboration with institutions in their own countries."

WARDA's intentions were unambiguous from the start. WARDA was not to be open in the sense of simply offering hospitality to scientists from the region or beyond who might wish to work there. "We did not want WARDA simply to become a roof and an administrative support structure for northern institutions to outpost people here to carry out activities which are their priorities. There's a danger of doing that. Other international centers have, in fact, opened up their centers in the past to a lot of people coming in whose work is not a priority of the host center."

One version of an open center is ICRISAT's Sahel center outside Niamey in Niger. The Sahel center, which was established in the middle 1980s, operates on a larger scale and accommodates scientists who are not necessarily executing work that is part of the ICRISAT program. "That's just another model," says Matlon. "We couldn't afford to do that. There isn't enough space or administrative support. So whoever comes here has to work as a member of our team on priorities we've identified."

Speaking in 1996, Matlon conceded that running the open center requires careful managing. Work that a candidate intends to pursue must be negotiated with WARDA in advance and fit the priorities identified in WARDA's strategy and its medium term plan. These individuals are expected to work as full members of WARDA project teams, not independently. "We have mechanisms in place to help us select the person who is outposted," said Matlon. "At least, we have to approve the person and in some cases we've screened CVs and indicated preferences on a short list. We also participate in the evaluation of the individual while they're here. So it's really a win-win situation. "If you look around now at those we call collaborative scientists here under the open center construct, about 40 or 45 percent of our scientists are collaborating scientists," says Matlon. "I think that through the open center and the collaborating scientists we clearly achieved critical mass."

Joint Endeavors

Integration of individual scientists into WARDA programs is not the only way the open center works. WARDA also provides a base for joint endeavors by regional and international organizations pursuing activities compatible with WARDA's research aims. Here too the criteria of partnership and comparative advantage rule.

An early example that Matlon says comfortably fits the WARDA model of the open center is the Inland Valley Consortium. The long form is the Consortium for the Sustainable Use of Inland Valley Agro-Ecosystems. Inland valleys, or *bas fonds* in French, are small valleys typically found in the upper reaches of river system tributaries. Runoff concentrates in bottom lands during the rainy season, providing moisture for a longer growing period than in upland areas so that the impact of drought is less intense. Lowlands also tend to be less vulnerable to soil degradation than the fragile uplands.

Inland valleys are a common feature of West Africa's characteristically rolling terrain, covering an estimated 50 million hectares in the region. A substantial part of these inland valleys is not farmed, however, because of conflicts over land use, difficulties with water management, health risks and agronomic problems such as iron toxicity and plant diseases.

Nevertheless, the productive potential of these lowlands offers a strong incentive to develop them and has attracted the interest of both national and regional organizations. The consortium began operation in 1994 and by 1997 was made up of 10 West African countries (Benin, Burkina Faso, Cameroon, Côte d'Ivoire, Ghana, Guinea, Mali, Nigeria, Sierra Leone and Togo), three CGIAR centers (WARDA, IITA and ILRI), France's Center for International Cooperation in Agricultural Research for Development (CIRAD) and the Wagenengin Agricultural University and the Winand-Staring Center for Integrated Land, Soil and Water Resources in the Netherlands. A small coordinating office for the consortium is located at M'be and each WARDA member country has a national coordinating unit to which participating institutions in that country belong.

As for how the consortium relates to WARDA's open center, Matlon noted that, in a sense, it is a reversal of the scheme in which individuals from other institutions work in WARDA projects. "WARDA is a member of the consortium. So we have roles to play and outputs to produce within the consortium. And the consortium's being based here gives us a marvelous linkage mechanism to a lot of other institutions in the region that we would otherwise not be working with in an area which is of the highest priority to WARDA—the development of inland valleys."

In an open center appointment, Jean-Yves Jamin of CIRAD was assigned as a coordinator to the consortium office at M'be. According to Jamin, the central aim of the consortium is to find practical ways to promote the intensification of inland valley agriculture through the management of water and inputs of fertilizer and other agricultural chemicals. Intensification is feasible in the inland valleys because dependable levels of moisture in the soil and higher levels of fertility there justify the investment.

No Big Dams

Jamin says that the consortium is not promoting the sort of large scale development of irrigation that was emphasized in the 1970s and 1980s in West Africa and was based on construction of big dams. These projects were expensive and not well adapted to the topography of the inland valley part of the continuum. "It is necessary to have-low cost schemes for the *bas fonds*, low-cost water control technologies and agronomic technologies," says Jamin. "You can't think of agronomy separate from land and water management." Many inland valley sites need improved water control. This means creating small dams and reservoirs and using bunds (earthen ridges) to contain water.

The consortium is committed to the view that the technical aspects should not be separated from the social and economic aspects of its activities. It is the latter that drive development, says Jamin. "If farmers can't manage a new system, it is of no use. We say do it only if farmers are interested and can find funds."

The consortium does not develop technologies. Plenty are available, says Jamin. Technology testing and technology transfer is the consortium's main function. Practicality at the farm level is emphasized. A main concern is that a technology being transferred fits the particular ecosystem in question. As the consortium began selecting research sites in participating countries it was logical to start by working out methods of site characterization and then to proceed to research on land development. Characterization covered not only hydrology and agronomy but also study of the economy, social organization and health issues at a site.

Because it strives for a "holistic" approach, the consortium emphasizes an interdisciplinary effort by the scientists involved. "We want people to work not as individuals but as part of interdisciplinary teams," says Jamin. Disciplinary cooperation is actively encouraged and rewarded, for example, in funding decisions. But the interdisciplinary ideal is not always achieved. "In principle, everybody accepts," says Jamin, but in practice interdisciplinary work is sometimes hard to organize. "We have to backstop it," he says.

Jamin cites two operating principles of the consortium. The first is to find ways to "help everybody to participate," the poorest countries included. The second is the principle of comparative advantage. Among the international institutions, for example, WARDA could give support for rice technology and CIRAD, hydrology. The participating countries are also expected to be active according to their capabilities. But it doesn't always work that way. Jamin acknowledges that some countries with more dynamic and better-developed economies are less engaged. Côte d'Ivoire, for example, has a more advanced agriculture than many of its neighbors and is not keenly interested in low- cost technology. Countries with greater difficulties are more active in the consortium, says Jamin.

Other challenges await. High on the list of consortium objectives is to bolster interactions between NARS and international institutions, an aim that has frustrated other organizations. Relatively little has been done in exploiting inland valleys in the Sahel. To change that the consortium will be required to give special encouragement to countries that are among the poorest in the region and least able to take the initiative themselves. And promoting scientific exchanges between francophone and anglophone countries demands the bridging of an historical divide. In other words, the consortium is faced with classic problems of cooperation in West Africa.

Fostering Feedback

Another variation on the theme of collaborative or synergistic partnership at WARDA is the Research on Accelerated Diffusion of Rice Technology Program in West Africa. RADORT is a response to dysfunctional agricultural development in many West African countries. In theory, international research centers provide new technology, NARS adapt it to their countries' requirements and national extension services do the grassroots work of demonstrating the technology and convincing farmers to adopt it.

In practice, the delivery system too often breaks down. Government organizations are poorly funded up and down the line. In many cases, training is insufficient, management is poor and morale low. Extension workers are often literally immobilized by lack of vehicles and fuel. The international centers and NARS for years did not help matters by an inflexible attitude toward technology transfer, handing out improved materials without real understanding of the conditions in which they would be grown and, certainly, without consulting the farmers.

In recent years, the value of farmer participation has been acknowledged, but constraints remain. For example, even if WARDA itself had the resources to take a more active role in technology transfer, the CGIAR mandate against direct involvement in extension work discourages such efforts. However, by joining forces with other international organizations in a coalition that includes a range of public and private organizations in the region, WARDA hopes through the RADORT program to have a positive impact on the diffusion process.

As the name implies, RADORT is designed to speed up the adoption of improved rice technology by small farmers. The program brings together smallholders, community organizations, public agencies and nongovernmental organizations (NGOs) to work together on rice research and development. WARDA coordinates the program from M'be. The U.S.-based Winrock International Institute for Agricultural Development is the subcontractor and its staff in West Africa is mainly responsible for research, monitoring, and training activities. The UN's International Fund for Agricultural Development (IFAD) funded RADORT's four pilot projects in Senegal, the Gambia, Côte d'Ivoire and Nigeria.

RADORT's planners emphasize working with NGOs as well as government agencies. NGO's have been viewed as operating in a less top-down manner, being more flexible and offering a better link to farmers than government organizations. Winrock had previously worked through NGOs and the Peace Corps in successful on-farm projects in Senegal and the Gambia, including some aimed at women farmers. So RADORT could draw on that experience.

Reversing the Information Flow

Government extension agents in the region have traditionally been trained to transfer agricultural information by issuing instructions to farmers, not to listen to them and understand their needs. A main RADORT effort has been to develop a systematic way of insuring a reverse flow of information from farmers. Prescribing a change in attitude does not, of course, guarantee results. And RADORT puts heavy emphasis on developing new techniques and analytical tools to enable it to interact more effectively with farmers.

Two such tools are called Rapid Rural Appraisal (RRA) and Participatory Rural Appraisal (PRA). The approaches they follow are implied by their names. Nils Hanssens, RADORT coordinator based at M'be, says development organizations, including NGOs, have found that they could do with less data. The PRA approach is aimed at working with farmers to identify their needs in a short time. "The philosophy is that you don't need complete data—optimal ignorance is the catch phrase." The emphasis is on the qualitative rather than the quantitative, so elaborate questionnaires are not required.

Close observation of interactions in the field is important. It is useful to note, for example, if extension agents pay more attention to innovative farmers with the result that others are slighted. To identify groups that require particular attention, interviewers may walk through fields and ask that farmers be ranked according to wealth. Wealth ranking is used to stratify populations and target people, says Hanssens. "There is information you want to provide to a poor farmer or female farmer different from what you provide a wealthy farmer." In its first phase, RADORT selected a few key sites for research to identify constraints affecting farmers. It then looked for partner organizations willing to invest time and funds in a broader effort to find ways to unblock technology transfer.

RADORT is a sign of the times. Development agencies are giving more weight to economic, social and cultural aspects of the development process. They are looking beyond government institutions for help in reaching rural populations, in particular to community organizations and to NGOs, both international and local. The old WARDA treated technology diffusion as a one-way process and found that its offerings found too few takers. Now, RADORT provides a feedback mechanism of a sort that WARDA says it needs and promises to heed.

Peter Matlon

Peter Matlon's concept of partnership seems equally a product of his training in economics and practical experience in West Africa. He was in the early wave of social scientists who joined the CGIAR centers in the later 1970s and contributed to the group's becoming a much more multidisciplinary endeavor.

Matlon's path into international agricultural research and eventually to WARDA differed somewhat from the typical one for his generation. Many of his contemporaries in international development were introduced to it through service in voluntary organizations, the Peace Corps for Americans and parallel organizations for those from other developed countries. Their pattern was to follow voluntary service with graduate work that qualified them for posts in overseas development organizations like the CGIAR centers.

Matlon says that as an undergraduate in the foreign service school at Georgetown University in the 1960s he became convinced of the importance of events in the Third World. During his time at Georgetown he worked for a few months as a volunteer in a Crossroads Africa project to build an infirmary in rural Uganda and says that he was immediately smitten by this first Africa experience. Determined to get a solid footing in development economics, he moved on to a master's program at Princeton's Woodrow Wilson School where he came under the influence of Sir Arthur Lewis, a Nobel laureate in economics whose work emphasized the significance of the agriculture sector for economic growth in developing countries. While at Princeton, Matlon worked as a Ford Foundation intern with a Harvard team developing a 5-year plan for Ghana, an experience that he says intensified his interest in Africa.

Matlon then went to Cornell with the intention of doing another master's, this one in agricultural economics. He says he was convinced to stay on for a Ph.D. when it was pointed out that having two master's degrees was worse than having none since it suggests two unsuccessful tries for a doctorate. After spending two years living in a village in northern Nigeria collecting data for his Cornell dissertation, he says he was committed to working in Africa.

Having completed his Ph.D. in 1977, Matlon spent two-and-a-half years as a junior faculty member at Michigan State University in the late 1970s, but says he kept looking for a way to get back to Africa and to work in technology development. The opportunity arose when he gave a paper at a meeting and an ICRISAT staff member in the United States at the time asked Matlon if he would be interested in the economist's position that was then open in Ouagadougou, Burkina Faso. And, says Matlon, "It all fell into place."

An Opening in Ouagadougou

Joining ICRISAT in 1979, Matlon proved himself a productive researcher and made a reputation as an economist whose work was well grounded in the agricultural sciences. Matlon says he had gone to Cornell because of its strengths in agriculture and took or audited basic crop and soil science courses in order to "at least understand the principles and know the jargon." He says that a major lesson he learned working at ICRISAT and later at WARDA was the importance of "the marriage of the technical with the socioeconomic. Either one in isolation didn't make any sense at all."

For ICRISAT, Matlon launched an ambitious on-farm research project involving 150 farmers in six villages in three agroclimatic zones in Burkina Faso. As part of the study, farmers tested new technologies on their farms. Year after year, technologies that flourished on research stations performed poorly in farmers' fields. Matlon concluded that a new research paradigm was needed in which farmers participated actively in the design and development of new technologies rather than just passively testing them. One corollary was that researchers would have to spend more time out on the farms and work with farmers as partners.

Matlon grew restive at ICRISAT's reluctance to move in this new direction. He had joined the center at a time when the CGIAR was still working on a paradigm of technology transfer, in ICRISAT's case with germplasm transferred primarily from programs in Asia. "As for the idea of developing technology in place with a high use of local germplasm, and trying to design technology that fit poor farmers' conditions, that just wasn't being done then." Matlon was convinced that much more interdisciplinary work was essential and that the international centers could not succeed in isolation. To close the circle with farmers it was necessary to bring national and international scientists into active partnership.

What made Matlon a strong advocate of a new sort of cooperation between national and international scientists he sums up by describing an encounter when he was arranging a workshop to launch ICRISAT's West Africa sorghum network. The plan called for a steering committee made up of national scientists. Matlon recalls a visitor from ICRISAT headquarters who was reviewing the program saying, "Why do you need a steering committee of national scientists? There's no need for that. It's our money that's running this network,not theirs."

Matlon says that by the second day of the meeting it became clear that such a steering committee was crucial politically if the network was to function and the idea was adopted. This occurred in the early 1980s, but Matlon says it was typical of an attitude toward collaboration that persisted. Out of experiences like that came the impetus for the WARDA task forces in which NARS scientists participate fully in setting goals and making operational decisions.

Matlon's experience had also persuaded him that it was unwise for ICRISAT to continue to invest as heavily as it had on crop improvement work for marginal growing areas, on millet in particular. He favored greater attention to crops more responsive to inputs in zones that offered higher production potential. He says that his efforts to convince people at ICRISAT of these views were making little headway and when the post at WARDA came up the shift was easy to make philosophically. WARDA would be focusing on a high potential crop in higher potential areas. And in Terry Matlon would be working with a director general whose approach to partnerships was strikingly similar to his own.

"Rice gardens" planted at one month intervals permit comparisons of growth and yield. Results enable WARDA scientists to integrate data into the RIDEV computer model to guide extension workers and farmers on optimal planting dates.

Crop modeler Michael Dingkuhn (right) works on the RIDEV planning and training tool for research, development and production with Abdoulaye Sow.

WARDA director of research Peter Matlon (at left) and board members in discussions in test fields. Rice breeder Monty Jones is at right.

Research director Peter Malton presents the Director General's Ebony Daba (farmers hoe) Award to M. Zongo Dramnane (left) for best WARDA male field worker and to Mme. Doni N´dri Francoise (right) for best female worker.

5 Agriculture and Health

Assessing the Risks

WARDA's partnership ventures are not restricted to research in agroscience and the socioeconomics of rice. Casting its cooperative net wider, WARDA and its partners embarked on an effort to appraise the consequences of agricultural development for human health.

In the 19th century and before, tropical diseases earned West Africa a bad name as the white man's grave. Survival time of European traders, missionaries and military men in the coastal countries averaged less than a year. Yellow fever, malaria and various enteric ills were the big killers, and many perished of nameless fevers. In the 20th century, medical science improved the odds for those who could afford its benefits, but high infant mortality in the population at large keeps average life spans in the region short compared with developed countries.

Today, sub-Saharan Africa is regarded as an incubator and potential exporter of dread disease. Indications that the AIDS pandemic got its start somewhere in Central Africa and high-mortality outbreaks caused by Lassa fever and the Ebola and Marburg viruses have convinced many that so-called emerging diseases pose a global threat. Population growth in Africa has spurred the sort of economic development—road building, deforestation, irrigation projects—that creates new habitats for the vectors and brings people without immunity into contact with disease. It is widely assumed that environmental change caused by these activities seriously increases health risks for humans. Surprisingly, however, little is known in a systematic way about the dynamics.

WARDA has a strong interest in finding the facts in the matter. Its strategy designates lowland areas as the part of the upland\inland valley continuum with the greatest potential for increasing rice production. Exploiting the lowlands, however, also means increasing human exposure to standing water and that, unfortunately, is viewed as entailing higher health risks.

To better understand the effect of agricultural development on water-borne diseases WARDA and six research institutions in the region in 1995 formed a health consortium, with WARDA serving as the base. Canada's International

Development Research Council (IRDC), the Danish Agency for International Development (DANIDA) and the government of Norway agreed to finance the project.

By taking a role in the consortium, WARDA was venturing outside the normal boundaries for an agricultural research center. Research on development issues has traditionally been compartmentalized. Because of development agencies' funding patterns, there has been little interaction between researchers in different sectors such as health and agriculture. Separatism has been very marked even within tropical disease research where the practice has been to support "vertical" programs concentrating on single diseases.

The major questions the consortium set out to address are whether promoting rice cultivation in lowland areas increases the frequency of vector-borne diseases among farming populations in those areas and whether water control projects for lowland rice cultivation increase the risk of disease. As "indicator diseases," the consortium focused on malaria and schistosomiasis because both are vector-borne diseases associated with stagnant water and have important health and economic consequences. The object was to evaluate the impact of different types of rice development on the risks of contracting these diseases. The information gained would make it possible for the consortium to map human health risks in major portions of the region, an output that would keenly interest policy makers. This would make it possible to design a strategy that would take into account agricultural and social welfare as well as health aspects of the problem.

A Broad-Spectrum Prescription

A broad-spectrum approach suited the project coordinator, Thomas Teuscher. A physician, Teuscher has had a long interest in community based medicine and experience that gives him ample knowledge of African rural society. Born in the United States, he grew up and was educated in Switzerland. The path he chose as an expatriate medical man in Africa put him on a trajectory toward the post at WARDA.

The top priority for the consortium was to "come up with outputs that are useful to policy makers," says Teuscher. To this end, the consortium planned to map disease, said Teuscher, "that is, to identify areas where you could expect disease rates to be high, low." In order to gain a better understanding of how rice cultivation and water control interact to affect the incidence of malaria in lowland areas the consortium initiated comparative studies in three major rice growing zones, the humid forest, savanna and Sahel. Twenty-four villages in each zone were chosen representing a variety of water control and agricultural systems—single and double cropping for example. Scientists gathered data year around on such things as numbers of infective bites by mosquitoes and new malaria cases.

Early results yielded some surprises. Evidence that expanding rice cultivation with the accompanying water automatically means increased malaria is proving to be far from clear. Variables such as the lifespan of mosquitoes in the area and even land preparation and application of agricultural inputs appear to be significant factors. Although certainly not conclusive, the research suggested that the intensification of rice cultivation in lowland areas is unlikely to seriously increase the risk of malaria in the forest or savanna. In the Sahel, expansion of irrigation may well increase the risks, particularly for people lacking immunity who migrate into the area. But this may not apply in the longer term. Teuscher says that knowing how much the environment adds to the endemnicity of disease in particular areas is crucial, "because control measures can only be successfully deployed in certain endemnicity settings."

Hopes for Intervention

On the question of whether the WARDA project can make a significant impact on health through work on intervention, Teuscher takes a cautious line. "It is a fact that in sub-Saharan Africa the area without malaria or without schistosomiasis is very restricted," he says. "Initially one hoped for interventions linked to management of the environment that would allow us to manage better vector-borne disease. I think I could show that (in a place) like the Sahel, where everything's dry and you add water, one could dream maybe of doing that. But in general settings in the savanna and the forest this probability is much lower." This is because the prevalence of disease is so much higher in wetter areas.

"Unfortunately, we don't have tools that work everywhere. If we can identify areas where more water will not add more disease that's good. But it might be that there are areas where diseases are entirely endemic. There we must think more about how could rules be developed to fit local farmers to cope better with disease.

"Right now one could say, well, there's nothing new, just diagnosis and treatment," says Teuscher. Diagnosis and treatment, however, can be improved. He acknowledges that the government health services on which most rural Africans rely have limited resources, but says small scale services can be made more effective particularly with the provision of clear guidelines and better health education for rural people. Basic steps to reduce exposure to the disease vectors will help. For example, use of bednets impregnated with insecticides has proved helpful against malaria and simple sanitation measures deterring people from contaminating snail habitats with human waste can reduce schistosomiasis infection.

Persistent Parasites

Both malaria and schistosomiasis or bilharzia are parasitic diseases for which preventive vaccines do not currently exist. Two types of schistosome infections afflict humans, urinary and intestinal schistosomiasis. Both types are endemic in West Africa. Humans are generally infected when they enter water and the larvae of the parasite penetrate the skin. A type of freshwater snail is the intermediate host for the disease. The severity of the effects depend on the number of eggs and the resulting burden of worms in an individual's system. Effective drug therapy for schistosomiasis is available and in recent years drugs of lower toxicity have been developed. But government health services in sub-Saharan Africa are overburdened and poorly funded and in rural areas treatment is often unobtainable. Also, there have been reports that the parasite is developing drug resistance.

Schisto primarily affects rural populations who encounter the parasite in the course of normal activities in farming, fishing, bathing, washing clothes, etc. The disease is not the outright killer that malaria can be, but it heavily affects children and young people and is a major cause of absence from school. In adults, it is debilitating and cuts productivity. Untreated it causes organ damage and chronic illness and is regarded as a contributing factor to death from other diseases.

In the case of malaria, the resistance of the parasite to drugs and of the mosquito vector to pesticides are growing problems. Malaria causes an estimated two million deaths a year globally, half of them among African children. The disease is thought to have originated in Africa and spread worldwide where conditions allow the vector, the female *anopheles* mosquito, to flourish.

After World War II, campaigns against malaria based on pesticide spraying and antimalarial drugs made substantial inroads against the disease, though less so in Africa than elsewhere. Hopes of eradication of malaria went glimmering as both mosquitoes and parasites developed resistance and problems of funding and organization hobbled the effort. Globally there was a shift in policy from eradication to control aimed at reducing the immediate impact of the disease. Longer term, hopes are placed in development of a vaccine.

The malaria parasite, *Plasmodium,* like its schistosome counterpart, has a complex life cycle. In humans, it begins when an infected mosquito takes a blood meal releasing sporozoites into the victim's bloodstream. Of the four species of malaria affecting humans, *Plasmodium falciparum* is the most deadly. In *falciparum* attacks, infected red blood cells cluster together and adhere to the walls of blood vessels, retarding the movement of blood. When the flow of oxygen to the brain is blocked, the result is cerebral malaria, which is often fatal. The resurgence of malaria seems to have followed a pattern of progressively more resistant forms appearing first in Southeast Asia and South America, but being carried inexorably to other congenial climes by mobile humans and, perhaps, stowaway mosquitoes. West Africa has benefited briefly from the lag, but the more virulent versions of *falciparum* are now present in virtually the whole region. Early treatment is essential. With children and others lacking acquired immunity, the disease can kill within 18 hours after symptoms first appear.

Waiting for a Vaccine

For people living in rural areas in West Africa, a Darwinian filter prevails."If you survive the first five years of life, you don't have to worry too much about life-threatening malaria," says Teuscher. "You acquire some immunity. That's why life expectancy at year five jumps dramatically. Everybody talks about a 45- or 50-year life span here. It's because under-five mortality is so incredible."

In places like Bouaké the epidemiology is different. "If you live in an environment where endemnicity is relatively low—in towns it is much lower than in rural areas—your immunity wanes rather quickly and you become susceptible, like a European. Which means frequent illness, fairly long illnesses and mortality is possible," says Teuscher.

For Europeans and other expatriates living in Bouaké this poses a dilemma. The practical choice is whether to take an antimalarial drug to try to head off the disease or to treat it when symptoms occur. Most short-term visitors choose the chemoprophylaxis option even though the side effects of the drugs currently effective against *falciparum* can be unpleasant or worse. Residents face a different equation. Many are reluctant to risk the long-term effects of a preventive drug regimen and play a waiting game.

"If you live in endemic country," says Teuscher, "one strategy not highly recommended, but still a reasonable strategy, is to treat any illness, not only high fever and chills, with a course of antimalarials. If you live for five years in such a place you'll do that 8, 10 or 12 times. But the total load of drugs will be much less." Teuscher practices this method himself and notes that there are ways to improve the odds. The peak period of activity for the *anopheles* is from 10 p.m. to 4 a.m. so it helps if you wear insect repellent outside and sleep in an environment that is protected by screens, curtains, and mosquito netting impregnated with insecticide. Air conditioning is useful not only because mosquitoes dislike lower temperatures, but because it means everything is closed up tight.

Teuscher adds that even the most careful precautions don't guarantee complete protection. "If you have a mosquito who is extremely hungry it will probably still catch you. But the probability is much lower." Whatever a person's recent medical history, says Teuscher, it is wise in malaria country to have an antigen test and take medication once a year.

Bouaké has a reputation as a malaria hotspot, but Teuscher is characteristically careful about putting all the blame on *Plasmodium*. "Febrile disease is a big threat in reducing the quality of life for most people here. I'm a little bit astonished that Bouaké seems to have more than most places in Africa. I'm not clear about endemnicity in Bouaké," said Teuscher, and his methodolgical inclinations take over. "I would like to launch a very small experiment, in different parts of town, to see what proportion of infections are malaria related and what aren't."

Is it possible to get effective treatment for malaria in Bouaké? As is usually the case in Africa, the answer has an economic dimension. "If you have money you can go to a clinic which has extremely sophisticated antigen detection tests. Within five or ten minutes you have a diagnosis of *Plasmodium falciparum* malaria. Or there is surely a pharmacy open where you can buy any of the latest European drugs. That is valid for perhaps ten percent of the population," says Teuscher. "For everybody else there is one place to go—the university hospital outpatient clinic, which gives low cost or no cost care. The whole town drains into a single hospital. But most people say 'I have malaria, I go to the market, I buy my drug, I take it.' The treatment is often too short, or the dose is not necessarily appropriate."

Professionals at WARDA are in the fortunate ten percent with access to the best care that Bouaké has to offer. They also have entree to a clinic in Abidjan four hours away that is said to rank as world class in the treatment of infectious diseases. Most people at WARDA seem to regard malaria as a manageable occupational hazard. Like other residents of Bouaké, they have, so to speak, learned to live with malaria. As for hopes of vanquishing malaria and schistosomiasis in West Africa, it is a matter of waiting for effective vaccines.

The protean parasites have so far frustrated the researchers and it is evident that a post-malaria, post-schistosomiasis millenium will be delayed well beyond the temporal one.

Thomas Teuscher

After Thomas Teuscher completed medical school in Berne, he took up a one-year internship at the Albert Schweitzer hospital at Lambarene, Gabon, with which his university had long standing ties. When Teuscher was at Lamberene in the early 1980s the house of the sainted medical missionary-musician-philosopher was maintained as a shrine. A place was set at the table for him every day, says Teuscher. Preserving the Schweitzer mystique helped raise money to run what was essentially a European hospital in the middle of the rainforest.

Teuscher says that his choice of Lambarene was purely accidental. He had taken a qualifying examination to go to the United States, thinking that completing his pediatrics training there would be a good way to get a sense of life in America where he had been born. He detoured to Africa when a colleague, who had worked at Lambarene, encouraged him to seek the internship there. Teuscher says he simply thought it sounded interesting enough to change his plans.

From Lambarene, Teuscher returned to Switzerland to continue training in pediatrics in Geneva. For his thesis, he designed an intervention project on sickle cell anemia in which he had become interested while he was in Gabon. He returned to Africa and carried out a year-long project at a hospital in Togo. At the same time, he was involved in a study on how to manage acute sickle cell anemia episodes.

His initial assignments in Africa gave him clinical experience, but even at that stage he says his interests were trending toward research, particularly research that would assist communities to gain better health. After Togo, Teuscher says he felt the need for further training in his area of interest. Because there was no curriculum for community-based medicine extant at the time, he gravitated to the London School of Tropical Hygiene and Medicine and signed up for a one-year course in clinical tropical medicine. That course gave him "all the basics," he says. "It gave me a very good base to understand the pathophysiology and etiology of communicable diseases. And also to see where we don't know much."

From London to Tanzania

Teuscher spent a further year at the London School as a visiting scientist working on a research project. He used nutritional data collected in Togo to explore the question of how food consumption patterns relate to communicable disease rates. At the same time, he says he needed to learn a lot more about epidemiology and being at a center of excellence made it possible to do so while he worked on the research project.

While in London, he applied for a post at a medical research center in southern Tanzania. Teuscher was hired as deputy director and, after a year, became director. Although a base for research, the place served also as a resource center for district health managers. Assessments of the quality and cost of care were done and a priority setting mechanism for health care was developed. The emphasis on health care planning led, for example, to the preparation of packages of essential drugs designed specifically for the districts in which they would be used. Previously, says Teuscher, "each district would get a standard kit. Each drug might be useful, but the amount of drugs needed varied among districts according to morbidity factors."

Teuscher says that part of his duties at the center was "to help transform it from a European style university-based institute to a member of Tanzania's medical research network." Also, he was expected "to identify someone who would take over my job, who would be an East African, ideally a Tanzanian." His task with the institute, he says was "to change it into something which much more responds to the way of managing institutions in a developing country." One important thing, says Teuscher, "we tried to break a bit the hierarchical thinking and way of managing by promoting an efficient team, which took many years to really assume authority and responsibility. I think in the end we managed to have an institute where, in the practical running, an able technician had as much weight as a Ph.D. student. It was a good experience to try that out," he says, to loosen the grip of "hierarchical expectations."

Teuscher stayed for six-and-a-half years. He says that in 1994 he heard that WARDA was looking for someone to manage a new health project and was tempted. The Tanzanian center was located on an inundated plain where rice was cultivated and during Teuscher's time there work was done on the efficacy of malaria interventions and on rapid mapping of schistosomiasis morbidity in order to allocate treatment resources. So he was familiar with a rice-growing environment and its problems. He applied for the consortium job and says that after a long hiatus while fund raising efforts went forward he was finally interviewed late in 1995. He got the job and moved to WARDA in March 1996.

6 Terms of Service

Expats and Indigenes

WARDA's concern about health clearly extends beyond its farmer clients to its own staff and their families. Health is one of the factors that influence how well a CGIAR center will be able to recruit and retain capable staff and be productive as a research institution over the long run. Other considerations obviously include such things as pay and benefits and also the amenities, or lack of them, where a center is located.

The composition of the staffs of CGIAR centers sets them apart from most other international development organizations that underwrite agricultural research. The latter typically operate by awarding grants and contracts that are implemented by other entities. A CGIAR center conducts its own research with its own staff. It does it with a mix of researchers and support staff recruited from developed and developing countries and this blend is a source of stress for the centers.

In the beginning, CGIAR scientists and administrators were drawn preponderantly from developed countries, prompting the charge that the CGIAR was a white man's club. The centers have made progress on easing the dichotomy between expatriates and others, but it has not been abolished nor has the resentment of what is seen as a double standard in hiring and pay. At WARDA, the main divide is between the small percentage of staff holding top research and administrative jobs, who are internationally recruited, and the much larger number of support staff termed General Services Staff (GSS). Most of the latter are from the region and their pay and benefits are much more modest than for international staff.

In recent years, a new category of WARDA employee has emerged to occupy an intermediate position between the international staff and the GSS staff. Known informally as regional professionals or regional hires because they are typically recruited in West Africa, they often have educational credentials (master's or Ph.D. degrees) similar to those of the international staff, but work under much less generous terms of employment. Fitting this group into the WARDA structure has not been friction free, but is seen by many as a necessary part of solving the larger problem of devolution.

The CGIAR prides itself on applying standards of excellence in recruiting researchers and excellence does not come cheap. Pay and perquisites for WARDA's international staff have traditionally been competitive with those of other international research centers and with development organizations in the UN system. The annual cost of an international staff member at WARDA in the middle 1990s averaged $120,000 or more. That included salary and fringe benefits such as pension and health plans and also allowances for housing and education for children, moving expenses, annual home leave, etc. Long-term staff members are eligible for a sabbatical leave for professional improvement after seven years.

On the other side of the ledger, international staff forego the sort of job security that university tenure or government service in developed countries commonly provides. They also have to be willing to work for extended periods in developing countries. For most WARDA staff members this means living in Bouaké. With 800,000 inhabitants, Bouaké is Côte d'Ivoire's second city in population after Abidjan, but is little known outside West Africa.

Bouaké lacks the grand boulevards, parks, official buildings and other amenities including a university center and four-star hotel and 18-hole golf course that President Houphouet-Boigny bestowed on Yamoussoukro, his birthplace 100 km to the south. (His intention of making it the country's administrative capital on the model of Brasilia, Islamabad and Abuja has not been pressed since his death.) And Bouaké ranks far behind Abidjan as a center of industry and culture.

Bouaké, however, lies in the geographical center of the country. It is a main crossroads of Côte d'Ivoire's national road system and a major stop on its north-south railroad, and is, therefore, a hub of passenger and freight traffic. In comparison with many African cities, Bouaké is well supplied with fruits and vegetables from farms in the surrounding area. Meat is slaughtered under Muslim dietary regulation and fish is available both from a large manmade lake nearby and shipped from the coast.

Bouaké has been a trading center with a varied population since precolonial times because the town lay on a main caravan route from the Sahara to the forest. Its citizens are drawn not only from other parts of Côte d'Ivoire but from many West African countries, particularly neighboring Burkina Faso and Mali. The residual French colony in the city is smaller than in the days of the post-independence boom but remains substantial and Lebanese families continue to form a visible entrepreneurial class as they do in many West African countries.

Different ethnic or occupational groups tend to cluster in separate sections of the city. A Muslim quarter, for example, is centered on the grande mosque.

But Bouaké has been comparatively free of ethnic or religious animosities and appears to have a lower incidence of criminal activity than many other large West African cities. Bouaké also has a reputation for a relatively pleasant climate with less rain, overcast skies, and breathless heat and humidity than the coastal areas.

Expatriate Life

A decisive influence on life at WARDA was an early decision not to build housing for staff and visitors at the headquarters site as did some CGIAR centers, particularly larger ones like IRRI and IITA. Cost was one consideration, but Terry makes clear that he was convinced it was preferable that international staff live in the larger community rather than in what would amount to an expatriate compound. M'be is a half hour's drive north of Bouaké and transportation is a major burden on the budget. Each international staff member is assigned an auto from the motor pool and low cost bus transportation to and from M'be is provided for other employees. No regular public transport is available.

Chitti Babu Buyyale is one who has no doubts that the arrangement is best for the institution and the staff. Not only does he note that building residential facilities at M'be would be expensive, but he sees the matter in terms of a practical equation. Now, only one member of a family makes the daily trip. If WARDA had housing at M'be, family members would still have to depend on Bouaké for schooling, medical care, shopping, recreation, etc., and that would "multiply the problem of transportation." And Terry and others suggest that there is plenty of evidence that being socially isolated is not a good prescription for harmonious relations in a small group.

Virtually all WARDA international staff live in the Kennedy quarter of Bouaké that in plan and architecture resembles other upscale residential sections in francophone countries in West Africa. The dwellings typically are roomy, high-ceilinged, one-story villas behind walls with guardians tending the gates at night. Kennedy, however, is not an expatriate enclave since there is a sizable Ivorian middle class, members of which are often the landlords of WARDA renters.

Bouaké is fortunate in having power and water supplies generally free of the interruptions frequent in other countries in the region, but public services otherwise are sparse. Streets in Kennedy are for the most part unpaved and, especially in the rainy season, the laterite roadbeds turn into deeply rutted torture courses for automobiles. On occasion, WARDA heavy equipment used to maintain the center's roads has been brought into town to make Kennedy's roads passable. The WARDA motivation, according to Terry, was less civic spirit than self-interest in preserving the suspensions of WARDA vehicles, which have to traverse the streets.

Most WARDA households employ a cook and guardian full time and some of them bring in daily workers for cleaning and laundry chores. Local wage scales are such that the total monthly bill for domestic workers is unlikely to exceed $300. Reliable domestic help gives the spouses of international staff members a measure of freedom, but they may encounter some obstacles to taking advantage of it. (WARDA international staff members were all men through most of the first decade in M'be.)

WARDA wives with credentials and experience that qualify them for challenging work discover that the job market in Bouaké is a lean one for them. Two-career families are not the norm in Africa; women educated beyond primary schooling are still by and large limited to teaching and secretarial level jobs. Some WARDA spouses learn that there is simply no demand for their specialties. One wife trained as a nutritionist, for example, found that occupation simply not recognized in Côte d'Ivoire. Wives who wish to work must be enterprising, and are likeliest to connect with freelance work such as translating or consulting. An anti-nepotism policy at WARDA imposes stringent time limits on the hiring of spouses. Sometimes, membership in the international community can provide opportunities. One scientist's wife with a nursing background took assignments that gave her experience in dealing with the medical and health problems of refugees, expertise for which demand is strong in Africa. As it happened, a majority of the scientists in the early hires by the new WARDA had young families and many of the wives chose the more traditional role of running the household and becoming involved in the community.

Occupational Hazards

Besides the increased hazards of illness and road accidents in developing countries, it is not unusual for the pressures of expatriate life to cause strains on marriages and problems with children. Parents worry about the effects on their children of growing up away from their home country culture and undergoing a very different socialization process. Schooling is a major concern. For English-speaking WARDA families, an obvious option is a school operated by American Baptists primarily for children of their missionaries in West Africa. A boarding school, it has a campus on the outskirts of the city with housing for students and staff. French language private schools, including a lycee, are also available.

Some WARDA international staff members send their children to their home countries to private schools or to live with relatives. The WARDA education allowance of $5000 a year per child falls far short of covering costs in most private schools in Europe and North America. A common practice is for children to be educated in Bouaké until they reach secondary school age and then be sent to their home countries to complete their schooling and prepare for college.

Peter Matlon followed this pattern when he worked for ICRISAT in Ouagadougou in the 1980s, sending his eldest child first to a French lycee for several years and then to the United States when she approached her final year in high school. He said Bouaké is an excellent place to bring up children if parents are satisfied with the level of education. He noted that local television had limited appeal and "children grow up reading and playing games and families talk to each other in the evening." (The advent of satellite television service, however, has affected the media mix). In the case of children who stay in Bouaké during their teenage years, he said that problems with drugs, alcohol and sex are less troublesome than in developed countries.

Professionally, Matlon says that for a scientist working in sub-Saharan Africa "to succeed in the long term, to stick it out and remain productive, the person has to maintain a level of curiosity. It's probably true in any research, but here that curiosity has to be driving his gut. I also think you have to stay committed to delivering a product that makes a difference in people's lives. You've got to believe that if you succeed in what you're doing people will eat better, have more income. That carries you through a lot of hard times."

There is no way to verify that idealism is a main motivation of WARDA researchers, but the evidence is that international staff are hard working and cope well with the considerable discomforts of field work and travel in the region. Certainly, they are expected to be productive scientists and will have short careers at WARDA if they are not.

Matlon acknowledges that patience will be tested. "You have to have a very good sense of humor, not let WAWA (the acronym for West Africa Wins Again) get to you, admire WAWA for coming up with a new one every time. Finally you've got to be culturally open, culturally curious, find something interesting in what other people might find frustrating." In short, there is no general prescription for flourishing in Bouaké. Matlon and others agree that the attitude the individual brings to the job and the life is most important. A fairly high proportion of international staff are married to partners from other countries they met at some stage in their careers overseas. These spouses also seem to have a talent for making the best of living in places like Bouaké.

No personality type appears to dominate among the international nucleus. However, there does seem to be a rough division between those who see their jobs as essentially focused on the lab and experimental field and a smaller number who take a broader interest in Africa. The former pay little attention to the culture or politics of the host country and spend spare time with their families and in the company of other expatriates. The latter more venturesome group tends to see more of West Africa on nonbusiness travel, seem more socially at ease with Africans, and perhaps take an interest in local languages, culture and history. In this category are mostly, though not exclusively, those without children.

Equity and Elementary Economics

The new WARDA in its first decade made relatively few regional hires, but the number is growing and their remuneration and status became an issue. Past circumstances are often cited to explain the disparities. When the CGIAR began operating in the early 1970s, poor developing countries claimed few holders of advanced degrees in agricultural sciences. This was especially true in sub-Saharan Africa. In those days, the CGIAR said it restrained its recruiting to avoid worsening the brain drain from these countries. The upshot was that international staff came predominantly from Europe and North America and, increasingly in later years, from Asia and Latin America.

By the 1990s, numbers of researchers from sub-Saharan Africa had been trained in both capitalist and socialist countries, owing at least in part to the stimulus of cold war competition. At the same time, the funding squeeze prompted the CGIAR centers to look for ways to reduce personnel costs and centers began to offer lower salaries to professionals hired from the regions in which the centers were located. Most CGIAR centers in developing countries now have some version of a two-tier system for professional employees. Large centers in Africa like IITA were able to establish employment categories for them more readily than small centers such as WARDA, where the few regional hires were suspended in a sort of organizational limbo.

Terry says that the WARDA managers were aware of potential difficulties, but started out in an ad hoc way, making a small number of regional hires when the center could not afford to add internationally recruited staff members for particular jobs. In almost every case, the results were awkward. Despite explicit cautions to the contrary, those who joined as regional hires expected, as time passed, to be upgraded to international staff status. When they were not some unpleasant encounters ensued.

As the budget pinch tightened, WARDA's board pressed management to explore recruitment of more people from the region for research and administrative positions. Developing an equitable system requires venturing into something of a personnel minefield. National agricultural research agencies in the region employ scientists with credentials like those of staff in the international centers. By comparison, the compensation of even regional staff in the international centers vastly exceeds that of NARS scientists. In very rough terms, WARDA regional staff members are paid half as much as its international staff, but at least twice as much as NARS scientists in the more affluent member countries and three or four times as much as those in the poorest countries in the region.

The differences in rewards have been a source of nagging resentment among NARS scientists. If anything, the disparity has grown as governments in the region reduced NARS funding as a consequence of structural adjustment reforms. Observers say that the feelings generated by the pay gap hinders cooperation between the NARS and the international centers.

Before Terry and Matlon stepped down, a start had been made in revising the WARDA personnel structure to accommodate a new category of professional with a package of salary and fringe benefits set lower than for international staff. The key difference is that these positions are not restricted to hires from the region. The first appointment of a candidate from outside West Africa was made in 1996 with the choice of a European scientist-administrator. Knowledgeable observers see this as a harbinger of major changes to come in the way WARDA is staffed and thinks.

Some risk is implied if WARDA and other CGIAR centers respond to budget pressures and demands for equity with major changes in their personnel policies. With a surplus of well-trained scientists in West Africa, it would appear to make economic sense for WARDA to stretch scarce funding by hiring more scientists from the region at lower pay and benefits than now go to expensive internationally recruited staff. And the argument is sometimes accompanied by harsh suggestions that by moving slowly the CGIAR centers confirm that they are elitist and racist institutions.

WARDA's reappraisal of the status of regional hires looked overdue, but caution seems to be in order. Any raiding of national programs for their best people would be counterproductive. Setting salaries too low could prevent a center from applying the criteria of excellence in hiring that the CGIAR sees as its trademark. Attempts at hasty "Asianization" or "Africanization" of center staffs could result in the loss of valuable connections to research institutions in developed countries that international staff have provided. This is not to say that change is inadvisable, rather that there are pitfalls to be avoided.

The Graduate Student Experience

In organization and spirit, WARDA is more like a university than a commercial research enterprise and does its bit to train the next generation of researchers. Although less than in a university department, graduate students and postdoctoral fellows do a good deal of the hands-on research at WARDA. But grad students, in particular, occupy a somewhat ambiguous junior status there. Postdoctoral fellows, on the other hand, usually come to WARDA to do well defined work on specific projects. Postdocs are further along scientifically than are most graduate students and, if they have good relationships with the senior scientists with whom they are working, things tend to go satisfactorily.

Recruitment of grad students is normally done by WARDA scientists in collaboration with the candidates' faculty advisers at their home institutions. The understanding is that a student's work will be relevant to a WARDA project. The experience of the large majority of graduate students at WARDA appears to be very positive. No one denies, however, that it is possible for a junior person to fall through the cracks. It can happen that a senior scientist at WARDA is very busy, frequently away, or not interested in the student's work. Or the grad student may not take well to the Bouaké environment or feel academically isolated. Such things happen in universities, but there are usually more options for support available.

As elsewhere, grad students at WARDA range from serious to obsessive about their work and have a flexible attitude toward time. A few lament that the rigid limits on the work day dictated by the schedule of buses that transport graduate students and lower paid staff to M'be from Bouaké may mean the untimely interruption of lab work. For graduate students, their in-between position can be awkward. For example, they may need equipment or software not available at M'be and can be caught between WARDA and their home institution in a tiff over financing its purchase. Field work is in most cases essential both to their thesis work and to the larger project to which they are contributing. Because of their status, their authority is seen as equivocal and this may cause difficulties in working with field assistants and observateurs, the latter being the staff members who keep track of developments in crop trials.

It is grad students and postdocs who tend to be critical of some members of the research support staff, grumbling about their unwillingness to work hard and take responsibility. A typical complaint is that, although support staff members have the scientific qualifications for their jobs, most depend on a supervisor to direct the work and, if the supervisor is not there, will not take the initiative.

If the support staff is not workaholic, neither is it irredeemable. One graduate student conceded that, although it took a year of his effort, the field staff members he works with finally did take an interest in his project and became very good at their jobs. Perhaps it is another example of WARDA's partnership principle at work.

WARDA management is aware that matters can go awry with grad students and postdocs. Recruitment and supervision of them was placed under the research department rather than the training department so that recruits would be unmistakably under the direction of the senior scientists with whom they are to work most closely. Management keeps an eye on the quality of junior-senior interactions and, if a problem arises, the matter is discussed with the senior scientist. Usually, satisfactory adjustments are made, but on a few occasions, management has intervened more forcefully. Junior researchers may encounter some local difficulties, but working in the WARDA setting with able scientists on high priority research topics offers them unusual opportunities, particularly if they are interested in future engagement in international agricultural research.

Prospects today for young scientists going on to make such careers are chancier than they were even a decade ago. The development business has been in recession since the 1980s and the reduction in official aid has caused a contraction in jobs. There continues to be a degree of mobility for researchers and administrators within the global agricultural research system made up of international organizations, government agencies, universities, non-governmental organizations, private contractors and consulting firms, and multinational corporations. However, if present trends persist, many people now working in international agricultural research will find that the system no longer has room for them.

Word from the Rank and File

Internationally recruited staff and collaborating scientists at WARDA are outnumbered roughly 7 to 1 by workers in support jobs. General Services Staff (GSS) positions range from low-paid guard and janitorial jobs through an ascending hierarchy of drivers, mechanics and clerical and craft occupations to upper echelons of research assistants and finance and administrative personnel.

In the summer of 1996, WARDA's GSS workers held a protest meeting in the center's dining hall. The occasion was an announced change in the morning schedule of the buses that transport WARDA's GSS workers between Bouaké and M'be. Many had long walks from their homes to the pickup points and objected to the earlier start that would be required. The meeting was the closest thing to a labor-management confrontation that had occurred since WARDA began operating at M'be.

Between 1988 and the middle 1990s WARDA enjoyed a period of placid labor relations. Not only was GSS pay generally above the market, but Côte d'Ivoire was experiencing serious economic difficulties. World prices of the primary commodities that are the country's main exports were low and unemployment was high. The country also underwent a political crisis at the time of President Houphouet-Boigny's death in 1993 that resulted in a slump in outside investment. And in 1994 a 50 percent devaluation of the CFA franc caused economic volatility that lasted for more than a year.

During this period, WARDA was able to hire and hold on to employees with technical and business skills that are scarce in West Africa. An indicator of this was the virtual absence of turnover. Then, however, the Ivorian economy revived, employment surged, and Abidjan, in particular, experienced a renewal of demand for office space and housing and the cost of living rose. As the economy improved, WARDA's location became a definite disadvantage. Ivorians with the skills needed by WARDA prefer Abidjan as a place to live and work. Employment opportunities are much ampler in Abidjan, the country's main job market. Personnel officer Simplice Kra notes that many WARDA employees have family and friends in Abidjan; some have spouses working there. And the appeal of schools, sports, religious associations, etc. in the metropolis is very strong.

In addition to the problem of the Bouaké location, the pay advantage of GSS employees had been whittled down. Gordon MacNeil recalls that when he joined WARDA as financial officer a pay scheme for local staff was already in place. WARDA was new to Côte d'Ivoire and the rates were based on those paid by USAID in Abidjan. The scheme was not well structured for an agricultural research organization and pay levels were substantially higher than those prevailing for comparable work in the local job market. As WARDA added staff, it became evident that it could not afford the rates and proceeded to ratchet them slowly down for certain staff grades.

The Market Catches Up

The first tremors of trouble for WARDA came in the mid 1990s in the form of resignations of hard-to-replace staff, such as bilingual secretaries, who left to take better paid jobs elsewhere. Labor laws in Côte d'Ivoire are modeled on post-World War II French labor legislation and are weighted in favor of lower paid workers. WARDA staff members in higher GSS grades, particularly those with research jobs, continue to be better paid than their Ivorian counterparts. With employees in lower grades, however, WARDA had lost its clear comparative advantage. In the words of one former WARD administrator, "The market caught up with WARDA."

The improvement in the Ivorian economy encouraged staff to be more active on issues of pay and status and, perhaps, provided them more leverage than they had in the past. But pay seems to have been a background issue in the summer protest. GSS employees indicated that the meeting occurred mainly because the changes in bus schedules were seen as an example of actions affecting staff being taken without any employee involvement. WARDA management was viewed as accustomed to making unilateral decisions on center operations and having them automatically accepted by the staff.

WARDA managers concede that the bus scheduling matter was poorly handled. The original schedule revision had been aimed at insuring that employees were actually on the job at M'be at the appointed starting time. Pickup times were to be advanced a matter of 10 or 15 minutes. After the protest, adjustments were made. Locations of pickup points were altered to accommodate workers who had long walks to their homes. The center subsequently completed the purchase of enough buses to transport workers to M'be in its own vehicles. Because of financial constraints, WARDA had been leasing buses rather than buying them. Workers had complained about the reliability and cleanliness of the buses used to transport them.

In broader terms, Terry says that he recognized that the staff was disappointed that more attention was not paid to their interests. For most of Terry's tenure as director general, WARDA's leaders were in a crisis management mode. Besides his involvement in planning and designing the center and setting WARDA's scientific course, Terry was heavily occupied in dealing with donors on funding and strategy issues and with WARDA's council of ministers and host country officials in establishing WARDA as a regional institution. With a lean administrative staff dictated by budget limitations, Terry relied on a small executive committee made up of department heads. By all accounts, his management style was to encourage an often extended airing of opinions on an issue, then make a firm decision and move on. Under these circumstances, Terry says that human resources development got less attention than was ideal and staff felt that they had been overlooked. In part because of this, Terry in his final year as director general got board approval to engage a management consultant to look at both remuneration and organization at WARDA and make recommendations accordingly.

A Clash of Cultures

Personnel matters at international agricultural research centers operating in developing countries have a special sensitivity stemming from relations between the center and its host country. A dimension that Matlon calls nationalism can seriously complicate center-host country dealings for the CGIAR centers. Not surprisingly, the centers are regarded by their host countries as prime sources of jobs. A great advantage Côte d'Ivoire saw in offering to provide a home for WARDA was that the center would generate employment for Ivorians. Some government officials have been quite assertive in applying pressure for the hiring of their nationals. At least twice, WARDA has been asked for an analysis of its employment rolls. Both times, host country citizens proved to be in a satisfactory majority.

Should WARDA's staff become overwhelmingly Ivorian, however, conflict could result. WARDA is, after all, a regional organization and it is important that it be able to recruit from the region. In fact, WARDA's regional identity gives it a degree of immunity to host country demands. Pressure to discriminate systematically in favor of employment of Ivorians would be sure to become an issue in the governing council, and that deters such moves. On the issue of favoritism, Matlon says, "WARDA's bottom line is that it's always trying to get the best people at the best value. If we demonstrate that we're fair and open and are not providing privileged access to WARDA employment it's generally appreciated."

WARDA has been watchful of its machinery for maintaining fairness. Ivorian labor law inherited a high degree of social protection from its French antecedants and is especially restrictive where firings are concerned. By law, GSS employees gain permanent status after four years on the job—after an initial two-year contract and a renewal for the same period. Job tenure is highly prized since it confers rights to health care, insurance, and pensions in a society where such benefits tend to be meager. In two cases on tenure disputes that ended in court, WARDA actions were upheld.

Employment is an arena where a clash of cultures can occur. WARDA is committed to respecting all aspects of Ivorian law, but the center's personnel policies are formulated in the northern mode with the interests of the institution given priority. WARDA operates in West Africa where the value system gives primacy to loyalty to family and friends. There have been instances where important people from outside have pressed WARDA management to employ relatives. WARDA managers insist that these candidates have gone through the normal employment process and there have been no exceptions to the rule of hiring the best candidate. In the past, there were some complaints of favoritism in hiring by the personnel office staff and efforts were made to safeguard the hiring process. For example, a board of three or four persons representing various sections of WARDA, is formed with each hire to pass on candidates.

Nevertheless, tensions over hiring and firing are likely to persist and employment policy for the WARDA work force to continue to be a sensitive issue. Such tensions are hardly unique to WARDA. They may well be inevitable in intercultural hiring situations where wide income disparities and different employment norms exist. And WARDA, in fact, has not experienced highly volatile incidents of the sort that have occurred at other international centers.

One Center, Two Languages

A source of divisiveness in the old WARDA was a mandated bilingualism. WARDA was formed on the principle that the member countries' interest in growing rice transcended the old colonial divisions that had separated West Africans into estranged groups whose official languages were English and French. When WARDA was established, it was constitutionally obliged to operate in a thoroughly bilingual fashion. However, the old WARDA polarized into antagonistic anglophone and francophone factions, which contributed to its decline.

At the new WARDA, there can be moments of incomprehension or irritation, but language does not appear to be a serious issue. It probably helped create a modus vivendi that the first group of scientists hired showed good facility in both languages. In the labs, the dominant tongue is English, the ubiquitous language of science. Because WARDA operates in a francophone country, a large majority of the support staff is much more comfortable in French than in English and many speak only rudimentary English, if that.

Fluency in two languages, in fact, is a requisite for the director general and director of research and others in upper echelon posts or in specialized jobs such as translator or bilingual secretary. In practice, for most jobs, knowledge of two languages is regarded as an asset but as a second order priority. If two candidates for a job are equally qualified professionally, the candidate more competent in the two languages is likely to be chosen.

WARDA complies rigorously with its bilingual mandate in its publishing program and conduct of meetings and training sessions. Other CGIAR centers must also communicate in languages that their clients understand; the difference is that with WARDA it is not optional. The cost of producing dual versions of all publications and of language interpretation is substantial, amounting to perhaps $200,000 a year. Sensitivities on language issues may be activated from time to time, and it is true that many of the farmers WARDA wants to reach speak regional languages and no English or French. But in providing a meeting ground for members of the governing council and board and especially for scientists from the region WARDA has done its bit to close the breach that history made between anglophone and francophone countries in West Africa.

7 Where Credit is Due

Prime Sponsors

The new WARDA has been fortunate in having a nucleus of donors who paid for bricks and mortar at M'be, supported the center steadfastly through its teething problems and, by and large, continued to back the center without forcing an agenda on it. Forming this inner circle of donors were Canada, France, Germany, Japan, the Netherlands and the African Development Bank. A subset of four of these--Canada, Germany, Japan and the Netherlands--also combined to pay off WARDA's debt contracted in financing its buildings.

Other donors have been important (See table page 122). Sweden, for example, has lived up to the Scandinavians' reputation as the most generous aid givers in per capita terms and has been a regular and unobtrusive patron of WARDA. Britain has been a reliable supporter of WARDA's crop protection work. And the European Community has made a strong contribution to WARDA's research on resource management. After donor contributions to the CGIAR stalled in the middle 1990s, the World Bank increased its share of support to encourage other donors and has been among the top funders of WARDA's basic budget in recent years.

USAID was the major backer of WARDA in its Monrovia period, but was of two minds about the center after the move to Côte d'Ivoire. USAID has a dual system of research support, with its global and regional bureaus exercising separate funding authority. The global program stopped supporting WARDA in its latter days in Liberia. Then, in the debate over revising CGIAR-wide policy on rice research in 1993, USAID formed a minority of one among donors in arguing that WARDA funds would be better spent through other centers. The Africa Bureau, on the other hand, has been a steady backer of the new WARDA. In particular it has been a mainstay in supporting the center's task force innovation. Through its first decade, however, the new WARDA's prime sponsors continued to be the donors who were the chief contributors to construction of the headquarters and development of the M'be site. Each has its own interests and style. Japan's affinity with rice made it a major WARDA donor before and after the move to Côte d'Ivoire. In addition to assisting with capital projects after the move, the Japanese continued to concentrate their

Grants and Contributions for the Year 1996 (in US $)

Unrestricted research agenda	**1996**
Canada	612 423
Côte d'Ivoire	304 616
France	105 508
Germany	397 921
Japan	1 497 116
Korea	49 980
Netherlands	295 299
Norway	170 121
Spain	30 000
Sweden	551 116
United Kingdom	187 890
United States of America	150 000
World Bank	605 000
Total unrestricted grants	**4 956 990**
Restricted research agenda	
African Development Bank (Institutional Support)	447 345
Canada (IDRC) (Vector-borne Diseases Project)	249 665
Denmark (Phytosanitary and Seed Health Project)	16 348
Denmark/IITA/TAC (Inland Valley Consortium Project)	151 759
Denmark (Vector-borne Diseases Project)	68 074
European Union (Crop and Resource Management Project)	725 328
France (Agrophysiology Project)	85 351
France (Inland Valley Consortium Project)	156 693
Germany (BMZ/GTZ) (Temperature Stress Project)	170 215
Germany (BMZ/GTZ) (Salinity Project)	27 876
Germany (GTZ) (Pesticides Project)	37 109
Germany (GTZ) (Soil Nitrogen Project)	36 642
IFAD (RADORT Project)	129 421
Japan (Grain Quality Studies)	70 000
Netherlands (Inland Valley Consortium Project)	393 010
Norway (Vector-borne Diseases Project)	84 925
Rockefeller Foundation (Anther Culture Project)	103 055
United Nations Development Programme (Training and Communications)	252 147
United Kingdom (ODA/NRI) (Weeds Project)	12 321
United Kingdom (ODA) (INGER Project)	245 011
United Kingdom (ODA/NRI) (Nematology Project)	28 886
United Kingdom (ODA/NRI) (Weed/Insect Interaction)	12 401
United Kingdom (ODA/CABI) (Gall Midge Project)	11 803
United States (USAID) (Rice Network Project)	473 186
United States (USAID) (Technology Dissemination Project)	163 012
United States (USAID) (Africa Link Project)	4 139
Miscellaneous	33 378
Total restricted grants	**4 189 100**
Total Grants	**9 146 090**

regular support on post-harvest technology--the processing, storage and cooking of rice--an area in which serious losses in quantity and quality occur in West Africa. Japan also has had a sustained interest in rice germplasm conservation and is now a leading backer of the program for development and dissemination of new rice varieties coming out of the Wide Crossing\NERICA project. The total of funds from Japan in 1996 amounted to about US$1.9 million, making it the largest contributor to WARDA's US$9.2 million 1996 budget.

The Netherlands has been a principal backer of the inland valley\continuum work and ranked second in 1996 among WARDA funders in total yearly contributions. WARDA has had a special link with the Netherlands' Wageningen Agricultural University over the years. Agronomist Louise Fresco there was a charter member of WARDA's reconstituted board and several Wageningen scientists have worked as staff members at WARDA or conducted collaborative studies useful to the center.

West Germany provided the new WARDA's first board chairman from outside the region, Heinrich Weltzein. In the early days, West Germany made an important material contribution by underwriting the heavy equipment needed for land clearing and road construction and maintenance. The bulldozers, etc., came accompanied by a technical consultant, Folker Hell, who oversaw assembling of the machines, helped set up garage and repair facilities and for over a year was de facto head of mechanical maintenance.

France's history in West Africa adds complexities to its relations with WARDA. France and Britain were the dominant colonial powers in the region, and the French maintained a strong commercial and political presence there after independence; the British, by comparison, largely pulled up stakes. Through the 1980s, France was the leading source of development assistance and commercial investment in the former French territories. French expatriate scientists continued to work in substantial numbers in both French research organizations and NARS in francophone countries. WARDA recognized that French scientists had produced a large body of valuable agricultural research and the French indicated that they were open to cooperating with WARDA. On each side, however, there was wariness about the other's intentions.

In the 1990s, the French government reduced the country's role in West African affairs and cut back development assistance. This meant withdrawing French scientists working in the region unless new arrangements could be made. The practical result was that French researchers at WARDA were paid from French government contributions to WARDA's central budget. Other donors have taken even more direct action by attaching strings to their funding, actions that some CGIAR insiders argue could seriously affect donor-center relations.

The Donors, Are They Owners?

A continuing question in international center operations has been to what degree the donors are owners. Donors can obviously exert influence over the centers by giving or withholding funds, but both sides over the years have recognized the advantages of striking a balance between maintaining the centers' cherished operating autonomy and satisfying donor wishes. Recently, however, donors have increasingly placed conditions on their contributions in ways that seem to threaten that balance.

As foreign aid budgets tightened, bilateral donors have more often tied funding to particular projects. The donors seem to be motivated in part by a wish to impose greater accountability and, consequently, greater efficiency, but also by a determination to insure involvement of their experts and institutions in development work. Britain, for example, created a new form of aid called "holdback" funding. Under this formula, a portion of UK support to the CGIAR was reserved to fund cooperation with NARS in the region or to establish links with British institutions.

Restrictions vary among donors. At the extreme is a bald requirement that scientists from the donor country sponsoring the project do the work. But there are exceptions. Canada, Germany and the African Development Bank are cited as donors appreciated for mainly providing support with minimum conditions. WARDA has had some success in diversifying its list of donors in order to retain flexibility in its budget and its leaders say it usually manages to reach mutually satisfactory terms in negotiating with donors on restrictions. But the tying of funding is seen as a growing trend and potentially serious problem for WARDA and other CGIAR centers.

At stake is the ability of centers to operate coherent research programs. That centers maintain control of budgets and, thereby, of programs has been a perennial concern for the CGIAR. When a funding crisis struck the CGIAR in the early 1990s, a major aim of the CGIAR under chairman Ismail Serageldin's leadership was to bolster unrestricted funding. And the World Bank interceded with a substantial infusion of funds for the so-called "core" budgets of the centers.

Targeted funding is unlikely to disappear as a fact of CGIAR life. It provides donors with leverage they would be reluctant to give up, and financing special projects has sometimes been the means of goading centers into making overdue changes. The centers themselves have a stake in special projects because attractive ones win donor support that might otherwise not be forthcoming.

There is a tipping point. If restricted funds come to dominate a center's budget, management will lose control of the program. WARDA has good reason to be sensitive to such a possibility. A major factor in the old WARDA's decline was that restricted funding grew to the extent that it destroyed the balance.

Timely Backing

Why has WARDA endured against the apparent odds? For one thing, the center was fortunate that key members of the CGIAR hierarchy provided backing at critical points. In retrospect, they qualify as godfathers to the new WARDA. After its rebirth in the mid 1980s, a fundamental task facing WARDA was to persuade doubters and detractors that its mission was worthwhile and that it was capable of performing it. Curt Farrar, who was then CGIAR executive secretary, and TAC chairman Guy Camus were instrumental in brokering the agreement that gave WARDA new life. Farrar also played a major role in convincing CGIAR members to provide the financial support that would give the revived WARDA a fighting chance. In the early 1990s Farrar's successor, Alexander von der Osten had a main hand in helping win acceptance of arrangements to pay off the loan that had enabled WARDA to proceed with construction of the center.

WARDA's board of trustees played a less visible but none-the-less important role during the decade of the center's rebuilding. CGIAR centers on occasion have drawn critical attention from the group, usually when a director general and the board found themselves at cross purposes. With WARDA, this did not occur.

For example, Terry recalled that the board was strongly supportive during the difficulties of the move from Monrovia and played an important part in the capital development of the center. He said that some members of the board were dubious that the Wide Crossing project would succeed, but soon revised their view and gave the project their wholehearted backing. Terry sums up his working relationship with the board by saying that throughout his tenure as DG the board was a reliable source of "wise counsel."

Chairmen regularly anchor board relations with center leaders because board members are far flung and may meet formally as infrequently as once a year. Four chairmen led the new WARDA board in the 1980s and 1990s. Moctar Toure was the first chairman and served for a year. Heinrich Weltzein was chairman from 1988 to 1992 and was succeeded by Henri Carsalade, who was interim chairman for about a year. Just Faaland took over in 1994 and steps down in 2000.

Faaland is a Norwegian economist who served as a director general of IFPRI and has extensive experience with the CGIAR. Speaking after Terry and Matlon left WARDA, Faaland noted that the CGIAR prescribes that a center should hold a full board meeting at least twice a year, but that it is not universally observed. “I do feel that it is difficult for board members to start again where they left off last time. Even with a six-month interval it is difficult. I try to remind everybody that we’re trustees throughout the year, not just when we meet. My feeling is that it succeeds and the board works very well.”

The pall of politicization that hung over the old WARDA still shadows WARDA. Faaland maintained that WARDA’s board mixing international and regional members functions without political bias. “By and large, regional members have acted as WARDA board members not as regional or country representatives. I think they have done this as much as I have coming from a donor country.” At the same time, Faaland says that WARDA’s link to the council of ministers of member countries “is also a very great advantage as it is now.”

He suggests as an illustration of the change from the bad old days the appointment in 1996 of a new director general to succeed Terry. To avoid any taint of favoritism, Faaland decided that WARDA board members should not be on the nomination committee and selected three qualified outsiders. Faaland says that when he discussed the process with the council, they suggested that the board come up with 2 or 3 nominees for the council to choose from. Faaland replied, “I can’t do that. We have to do that for you. Your responsibility is to say no if you don’t approve. Then we will have to start all over again.” The council acquiesced and a precedent was reinforced, but it was another proof that the new WARDA still must live with the legacy of the old WARDA.

Doubts Disproved

A skeptic who changed his mind about WARDA was TAC member and then chairman Alex McCalla. Before the climactic CGIAR showdown on WARDA in 1985, TAC on the whole was hostile to the center’s continued existence. McCalla acknowledges that he himself “was one of the most skeptical people of the whole bunch. I was convinced in the middle ‘80s that WARDA was a waste of money and should be closed. I grudgingly came to the conclusion that it had a program that looked credible. Because WARDA was on TAC’s agenda in almost every meeting for three years, I think it’s fair to say that, from beginning to end, by the force of their logic and their program they systematically won over TAC members one by one.”

When McCalla completed his term as TAC chairman in 1994 he moved to the post of director of agriculture and natural resources at the World Bank. Speaking in 1997 immediately after Terry and Matlon had left WARDA, McCalla agreed with other observers that the leaders of the new WARDA would never have gotten their chance were it not for WARDA's special character. "I think the reason WARDA survived was, first, the West Africans in the form of Mr. Sagna in 1985 saying, 'you racist Northern neocolonialists, don't tell us how to run our show.' The intergovernmental character of WARDA has been marginalized in terms of its importance to the operation, but it nevertheless is still an intergovernmental institution. I think that scared donors away from taking action that they might have taken if there wasn't that sort of colonial guilt heritage left around."

Secondly, he awards major credit to Terry and Matlon. "I think they did a superb job of planning. By force of necessity they built WARDA as a partnership organization in an era before partnerships were in," said McCalla. "I suppose it was them and their ideas that turned me and many other people around to say they know what they're talking about and should be given a chance. In my view they did an absolutely brilliant job of tapping the best scientific minds they could, of designing a program which was focused and had some chance to succeed.

"They knew they were never going to have very many resources--they weren't going to be an IRRI with a hundred senior scientists. So from the beginning they knew they had to build partnerships to get things done. That was an imperative for them to survive. But given what's happened in the research business in the way of building partnerships--bringing the NARS much more heavily into the research process--they put WARDA into the forefront of a collaborative kind of approach to research. They built a rapport with their country partners that I think really stood them in very good stead.

"Now, I think that when the CG went to more ecoregional kinds of research and programs that address natural resource management issues, again WARDA is well placed in the new program they've designed because they're interdisciplinary, they're collaborative. They've had good leadership and they've had a pretty good board and the ministerial council has basically abided by their agreement and stayed out of the management of the institute, And they've always had a core of strongly committed donors."

To all these positives, McCalla added a qualifier. "In any sort of reasonable research program you're not going to see results for 5 or 6 or 8 or 10 years. WARDA's still in the honeymoon period of having everything right in terms of what's on paper, what's being done; they have good facilities now, good relationships with national programs. And now they have to deliver."

WARDA scientists and farmers at participatory varietal selection session. Women form the majority of rice farmers in the countries of West Africa.

Eugene Terry

Kanayo Nwamze

WARDA was named winner of the 2000 King Baudouin International Agricultural Research Award at the CGIAR International centers week meeting. At presentation were (left to right) WARDA board member Dunstan Spencer, CGIAR chairman Ian Johnson and WARDA director general Kanayo Nwanze.

8 Postscript

A Change in Management

The sort of circumspection that McCalla evinced toward WARDA was not uncommon in the middle 1990s among informed observers who saw WARDA's promise but were uncertain about a payoff. Four years later such caution seemed unnecessary. In late 2000, the CGIAR gave WARDA its coveted King Baudouin International Agricultural Research Award for its NERICA development. This accolade followed an endorsement of WARDA's program and management in the external review that the CGIAR centers regularly undergo. External reviews seldom strike an expansive note, but among their conclusions the reviewers observed that "WARDA is well positioned to contribute more towards a rice-based green revolution in West Africa."

The King Baudouin Award, which carries a cash prize of $10,000, was created in 1980 with funds the CGIAR received when it won an international development prize given by the Belgian king. The CGIAR's Technical Advisory Committee chooses the winners of the award, which is made every two years to "persons or organizations, irrespective of nationality, which have made a significant contribution to the development of the Third World, as also to solidarity and good relations between industrial and developing countries and between their peoples."

In the four years preceding these endorsements WARDA was under new management. Terry's successor as director general was Kanayo Nwanze who took over at the end of 1996. High on Nwanze's immediate agenda was to deal with the recommendations of a recently completed management study. In Terry's last year as DG, WARDA's board had assented to bringing in management consultant, William Gormbley. Disquiet among GSS employees and the issue of regional hires were not the only rèasons for the reassessment. The feeling was that a decade had passed and the policies and procedures that had been designed for a new organization needed a thorough review. The terms of reference were that a broad look be taken at WARDA's pay structure and personnel rules. A report was submitted before Terry and Matlon left WARDA, but no decisions on the recommendations were taken that would preempt action by WARDA's new director general.

Kwanze said that the review was timely and he was pleased that it provided guidelines for making management changes. With board backing, he carried out several of the report's recommendations. The posts of director of finance and director of administration were combined, as they had been when Gordon MacNeil took over after the move to Côte d'Ivoire. A position of human resources officer was created to give human resources development issues sharper focus and a start was made in updating some policies for both international staff and GSS employees.

Nwanze and the board promptly followed the report's advice on formalizing the status of the loosely defined category of regionally hired professionals, now termed associate principal staff. Posts in this category are open to young scientists from any area, not only to those from the region. The new DG said he was in a position to understand the problem because he had experienced all phases of it. A Nigerian citizen, Nwanze began his CGIAR career in 1971 as a regionally recruited research assistant with IITA. Later, he returned to IITA as an entomologist on a postdoctoral fellowship. He subsequently won an internationally recruited position there as a scientist and ascended through the CGIAR ranks to become WARDA director general. An assignment in Zaire in the 1970s gave him the foundation in French required for the leader of bilingual WARDA and he acquired administrative experience when he was in charge of ICRISAT's Sahelian center while it was being developed in the 1980s.

Room for Growth

Along with organizational change has come expansion of the physical plant. By the middle 1990s, WARDA was short of laboratory space and, because of the austerities of its start in Côte d'Ivoire, lacked some facilities regarded as standard at other CGIAR centers. In 1995, the WARDA board approved a building plan that would provide additional room for research and also a new home for the center's information and training activities. By 1998, a decision had been made to go ahead on the building project by relying on core budget funds and defraying the cost over three years. Construction was completed in 1999.

The new labs and scientists' offices are housed in an extension of the main building that conforms architecturally to that structure. Space is provided for researchers in soil physics, hydrology, grain quality, and plant physiology and for a new cold room. The last is not a full-scale genebank affording long-term germplasm storage, but it replaces the small original facility and expands and upgrades WARDA's capacity for medium-term storage of genetic materials and accommodates the center's working collection for plant breeding work.

A separate building for information and documentation services was constructed close to the research building. It also contains space for training activities and conferences. The original WARDA library and training facilities were in improvised quarters at the upland center some 3 kms from the main building. The old facility's limitations restricted its usefulness to WARDA scientists and also its role in regional information dissemination.

Total cost for both facilities was US$1,625,000, with the addition to the research building costing US$900,000 and the information and documentation facility US$725,000. The funding plan was made possible by payments from member states, particularly Nigeria. The financial participation of the member countries has been greeted not just as a welcome solution to a current problem, but also as a hopeful sign for the future.

Away from the Status Quo

WARDA's prospects in the near term depend heavily on the Wide Crossing\NERICA program fulfilling its promise. In the longer run, WARDA's fate is tied to that of the CGIAR system. The CGIAR faces many uncertainties and there is broad agreement within the group that the status quo is not a satisfactory formula for the future. In 1997, a comprehensive review of the CGIAR system was launched to help map what were expected to be the most extensive changes in strategy and structure since it was established a quarter century before.

Driving the desire for reform are rapid progress in science and changes in the world economy. Advances in biotechnology, in particular, have confronted the CGIAR with a set of issues with which, in its present form, is poorly prepared to deal (See page 75). Critics outside and inside the group have also argued that the CGIAR organization is too unwieldy to set and pursue system-wide priorities effectively and that cooperation between centers leaves much to be desired.

In its early days, the CGIAR concentrated on crop improvement work directed mainly at increasing farmer productivity. In the 1980s and 1990s concerns about the environment motivated the group to emphasize sustainability in its work. It also responded to accusations that it was neglecting the interests of the poorest farmers in less-favored agricultural areas. To develop technology effective in such areas it was necessary to gain a better understanding of ecosystems and greater emphasis was placed on research on natural resource management. The group's priorities now are a trinity of germplasm management, poverty reduction and natural resource management.

Finding a formula to reconcile the divergent demands of germplasm management and poverty reduction poses a formidable challenge. Two ideas that shaped the discussion are adopting a federation model for a CGIAR structure and moving toward a regional focus in center strategy and organization. The debate on federation has turned on the question of greater or lesser degrees of centralization. By the time of the group's international centers week meeting in October of 2000 several competing variants of a plan for a federation had been put forward, but the outlines of a restructuring scheme appeared to be emerging.

Underlying the support for a federation was the sense that the CGIAR should become better able to deal with germplasm conservation and intellectual property rights issues. With the private sector increasingly active in the exploitation of genetic resources and the field becoming dominated by market forces the view was that the CGIAR's role as a major producer of "public goods" and a proponent of poor farmers' interests had to be bolstered. One proposal was for the creation of a CGIAR board, which would take the lead in genetic resources management and intellectual property issues and have greater authority in making policy for the system. Under most federation plans, other functions would be more centralized, including provision of common services, public information, fund raising and perhaps some personnel activities.

A Regional Rationale

The rationale for adoption of a regional focus is based on the perception that agricultural development varies so greatly in different regions that the global mandate under which the centers typically operate is unsatisfactory. As the argument goes, it is necessary to take into account not only ecology but the political, economic and social context in a particular region as well. A favored regional model emphasizes linking the centers more closely with a wide range of partners including governmental and non-governmental organizations, farmers groups, educational institutions and the private sector. Some observers note that this formula strongly implies that the centers would be more deeply involved in development activities as distinct from research. It is suggested that the regional model would require the merger or shutting down of at least some centers.

The reorganization under discussion would change the character of the CGIAR. The group has been reflexively loyal to its founding principles of center autonomy, maintaining a nonpolitical stance and making decisions for the system by consensus. The alterations being contemplated would require significant modification of these principles, a prospect that troubles CGIAR fundamentalists. At its 2000 Washington meeting the group resolved to develop a specific plan over the succeeding six months in order to begin the process of reform. Whatever plan is chosen, the transition will be neither quick nor easy.

WARDA enters this testing period with some distinct advantages but facing daunting challenges. The external review of WARDA presented to the CGIAR mid-term meeting in the spring of 2000 confirmed that WARDA is now regarded as a "mature" center. The accompanying cover letter noted that the review was "positive but critical. It shows that WARDA has transformed and emerged into a credible scientific institution with international leadership in rice research. Overcoming hybrid sterility barriers and the successful introgression of adaptation and tolerance genes from the wild African rices *(Oryza glaberrima)* into the high-yielding rices of Asia is a major scientific breakthrough in rice improvement." The letter signed by CGIAR executive secretary Alexander von der Osten and TAC chair Emil Q. Javier, adds, "This achievement at WARDA will have a major impact on rice production not only in Africa, but also in Asia and Latin America."

If the external review is "positive but critical," the positive far outweighs the critical. The negatives pertain more to the area of policy than of performance. The reviewers urge that WARDA's board be more involved in center leadership, particularly in guiding the organization in developing its strategy. They also say that WARDA needs to do a better job at demonstrating the impact of its work. This fits in with the CGIAR's concern in recent years about justifying center activities to donors by pointing to concrete economic results in developing countries rather than simply citing achievements in the abstract. In a related observation, the reviewers observe that a lack of continuity in WARDA socioeconomic research program has disrupted progress.

The external review also comments on "unfinished business" with staff morale issues. In the final months of Terry's tenure as DG an ad hoc committee of GSS staff members was formed to present the staff's case in the bus scheduling dispute. WARDA employees do not have a union and a guarantee of regular consultation with management was one of the issues under discussion. The ad hoc staff committee was dissolved in 1997 and a GSS Consultative Committee was established with members democratically elected. The committee has formal status in representing employee views to management. The external review, however, found that communication between senior management and staff is still "inadequate." Staff continued to be uncomfortable with aspects of the senior leadership's management style and with employment conditions and expressed concern about lack of recognition of personal achievement and about career prospects. In a joint response to the review, WARDA's board and management identified three major challenges "—more consultation for increased transparency and participation, attracting and retaining high caliber staff, and building and sustaining morale—challenges which will be addressed by the (senior management team) over the next 12 months."

Variable Roles

The external review cover letter notes,"WARDA has crafted effective partnerships with its stakeholders and represents a successful example of regional cooperation." If, as appears likely, the CGIAR moves toward a regional orientation, the role of the centers will necessarily vary from region to region. As described earlier, some national programs in Asia and Latin America are asserting their readiness to take over greater responsibility--and not simply for downstream research--and express impatience at what they see as the reluctance of the international centers to relinquish control. Accordingly, the centers are under mounting pressure from donors to hasten the transfer of functions to NARS that are up to the challenge.

In sub-Saharan Africa, however, NARS still require substantial strengthening. In addition to the need of NARS for institutional reform and better funding, observers suggest that a less overt difficulty inhibits West African national programs. This is described as a dependency relationship between the NARS and international centers. By this diagnosis, the international centers' superior resources in scientific talent, research funding, instrumentation, vehicles and fuel, travel budgets, etc., put them in the position of dictating to the national programs, thus discouraging the NARS from maturing.

WARDA's emphasis on partnerships offers a practical way to combat the dependency syndrome. Through its task forces, WARDA established a more collegial relationship with national program scientists and fostered interactions among NARS scientists from different countries, which helps break down barriers to regional cooperation.

Dependency to Devolution

Creation of a functioning regional research system is seen as of benefit to all national programs in West Africa and a means of giving a lift to weak programs in particular. The emergence in the 1990s of an entity called a subregional research organization (SRO) is viewed as a hopeful move in that direction. An SRO's main purpose is to help define a regional strategy in agricultural research and to coordinate such research in the region. Already in being are the Southern Africa Center for Coordination of Agricultural Research (SACCAR), and the Association for the Strengthening of Agricultural Research in Eastern and Central Africa (ASARECA).

SROs in Africa are still defining themselves and wooing donors for support. In West Africa, the *Conference des responsables de la recherche africaine* (CORAF) has established itself as the region's SRO. CORAF, was originally created and funded by France but has gained more broadly based support from other donors and wider membership by including anglophone countries, thus fostering the independent identity that is essential. WARDA has embraced CORAF by merging its task forces with CORAF's rice research and development network. A coordinating unit will be located at WARDA headquarters and a NARS scientist will coordinate each task force. The network will operate on the WARDA task force model with its emphasis on partnership. SROs in Africa and elsewhere are seen as stepping-stones to devolution--the CGIAR now prefers the term partnership--and development of SROs is likely to move up on the group's agenda if regionalization gathers momentum.

Partnership Equals Participation

In other ways WARDA under Nwanze has extended initiatives begun under Terry and Matlon. In 1996, leading rice-breeding institutions agreed to join forces to exploit the potential of interspecific hybrids. WARDA became the lead center of an international group that includes government research organizations from France and Japan and China's Yunnan Academy of Agricultural Sciences as well as CIAT and IRRI from the CGIAR and Cornell and Tokyo universities. Called the Interspecific Hybridization Project, the participants pool resources to work on common problems. The external review called the project one of the most successful partnerships at WARDA.

WARDA is also pushing a variation of partnership designed to accelerate technology transfer. It has been standard practice for a research center that has developed a promising new rice variety to send it to a national program for evaluation and approval for use in that country. Typically, this takes 4 or 5 years and several years more for the new variety to reach the farmers' fields, if it ever does. A scheme for bringing farmers into the process much earlier had been successful with other crops elsewhere and a decision was made to try what is called participatory research for rice in West Africa.

Two sorts of participatory research programs have been developed. One is participatory rice breeding in which farmers select individual lines from generation to generation in the breeding process. The other is participatory varietal selection. WARDA rice breeder Monty Jones says that the varietal selection program has had the greater impact in speeding the adoption of new rice varieties by farmers. The key to the program, according to Jones, is that scientists do not give farmers finished rice varieties, but rather ask them to help select and refine the varieties to suit their own preferences.

In the participatory program, researchers chose a particular community and plant a range of materials. These include traditional types as well as a clutch of interspecific hybrids. As the growing season advances, farmers mobilized from surrounding villages are taken to the fields. They are asked to move from plot to plot and to note their choices and the reasons for those choices. Jones says, "These criteria for selection we take into account in developing new varieties."

This process is repeated in three phases of the growing season including post harvest. The next year, 5 or 6 varieties that have been selected are given to each farmer with the idea that they will plant them and compare the results with their old varieties. When farmers are pleased with the outcome word spreads rapidly and the adoption of NERICA varieties has occurred much faster than under the previous system. From the start, emphasis has been placed on including women in the program because women constitute a majority of rice farmers in the region.

Participatory trials were launched in Côte d'Ivoire in 1996 and begun in Guinea and Ghana in 1997. By 1999, they were being carried out in 17 WARDA member countries. WARDA has been able to afford to conduct trials in only one community in a given country, with effectiveness varying from country to country depending in large part on the flexibility and supportiveness of governments. Guinea is cited as an exemplar where the government has given priority to the program, especially in backing the involvement of extension workers. The willingness of Guinean farmers to collaborate in matters such as exchanging varieties is viewed as another reason that the program has prospered there. Jones says that because of the practical benefits farmers perceive, Guinean farmers in 2000 were "rushing for the new materials." He estimates that "this year 40,000 will be planting them."

A major problem in many West African countries has been the lack of sources of affordable seed for improved varieties. WARDA has promoted and supported a community-based seed multiplication scheme to make it possible for farmers to buy and sell seeds in their own communities. Innovative farmers are picked and trained in seed multiplication. They meet at the beginning of the season to identify varieties worthy of multiplication and are given assistance if needed. Guinea, again, has been a leader in community-based seed multiplication.

When Mandates Collide

A choice of the regional option by the CGIAR would bring WARDA some opportunities, but also some risks. As WARDA has established its bona fides, it has been suggested that the center extend its geographical reach, that it might take on continental responsibilities for research on rice-based cropping systems. Such expansion could create intramural friction in the CGIAR. Cooperation among centers is encouraged, but competition is not unknown. Tensions typically occur when mandates overlap; such stresses are likely to increase as the international centers modify their missions. When intercenter rivalries have occurred in the past, troublesome issues have usually been resolved satisfactorily by the parties involved. As the CGIAR refocuses and center mandates change, however, the stakes may seem higher and disputes become more disruptive. And the CGIAR may have to intercede in jurisdictional and territorial arguments in ways that it has not in the past.

Since WARDA and IRRI share a mandate for rice research, turf disputes between them are possible. IRRI is one of the CGIAR's flagship centers. It is several times the size of WARDA and has a distinguished record of achievement. Based in the Philippines, IRRI has focused its work primarily on Asia. With Asian national programs claiming a greater role in research, IRRI is already looking for new horizons, geographic as well as scientific. Whether IRRI and WARDA operate as allies or competitors clearly has implications for the future of rice research in Africa

Nwanze said at the time of the 2000 Washington meeting that the WARDA board and TAC agree that WARDA's focus should remain West and Central Africa, noting that Cameroon, Chad and the Central African Republic are now members of WARDA or have requested to be admitted. He said that WARDA will not post staff outside West Africa unless and until demand occurs.

WARDA and the Future

Overhanging the future for WARDA and all the CGIAR centers is the question of whether the great expectations for biotechnology will be realized in the years ahead. However, a number of nonscientific variables will also weigh heavily in determining WARDA's fortunes. WARDA's character as an intergovernmental organization, unique in the CGIAR, is seen both as a source of both strength and hazard. On the one hand, WARDA has benefited from links with its member countries that other centers lack. WARDA has become an object of pride in the region, which greatly aids the center in building cooperation. On the other hand, ultimate authority over WARDA is vested in a council whose members are appointed by its constituent governments. Pessimists point out that the charter was not changed in this regard when WARDA was reconstructed in the 1980s and the potential for WARDA's being repoliticized persists. The governing council has abided by its commitment to noninterference and there has been no sign of backsliding, but any revival of politically driven behavior could put WARDA in jeopardy again.

WARDA's redefined partnerships are strengthening NARS in the region and assisting WARDA in meeting its own research agenda. Ultimately, WARDA's efforts at cooperation with national programs and non-governmental and private sector organizations are aimed at helping to overcome the shortcomings of infrastructure in West Africa and an economic, political and social environment that hampers agricultural development in the region. By striving to achieve regional balance in the working groups through enlisting equal numbers of members from English and French speaking countries and from the Sahel and the humid zone, some progress was made in overcoming divisions that have retarded cooperation in the region.

The literally bottom-line question is whether the donors will oblige by funding the CGIAR at levels sufficient to finance its ambitious new agenda. And will the governments of WARDA member countries give greater financial support to national research programs and refrain from political interference? Most fundamental, will the region avoid the sort of political volatility that led to the devastation of Liberia and Sierra Leone and appeared to threaten Côte d'Ivoire in 2000? Any significant upset of that country's enviable post-independence equilibrium would obviously have a serious impact on WARDA.

Terry and Matlon and their colleagues achieved stability and credibility for the new WARDA. And WARDA under Nwanze has built on those achievements. The challenges in the coming years will be different but no less difficult, stemming as they do from a range of political, economic and social issues that are critical not only for agricultural research and WARDA, but for development in general in West Africa.

Appendix

Rice Economics and Statistics

A Global Perspective

From the time WARDA joined the CGIAR there had been objections to its focus on a single region. The critics also argued that, by normal CGIAR criteria, the WARDA budget represented a disproportionate allocation of group resources to Africa since production and consumption of rice in Asia far exceeded that in Africa. WARDA was put to the test when the CGIAR Technical Advisory Committee commissioned a review of rice research across the CGIAR system to be completed in early 1993. The group complements its regular evaluations of individual centers with periodic horizontal looks at how the group as a whole is performing with respect to particular crops or regions. The aim of these so-called "stripe" reviews is to avoid duplication and promote coordination system wide.

The rice review was prompted mainly by concern that population growth would require a doubling of rice production over 30 years. Worries about a tailing off in the rates of increase in rice yields and an awareness of the difficulty of achieving higher production while maintaining sustainability added to the sense of urgency. Several CGIAR centers are directly or tangentially involved in rice research, but the focus was unmistakably on two, IIRI and WARDA.

The stripe review was chaired by Grant Scobie, a respected New Zealand economist, and the report, when it came in, reflected an economist's approach. As suggested by the title, "Investment in Rice Research in the CGIAR: A Global Perspective," the intention was to address global needs and indicate how the CGIAR could best help meet them with its tightening resources.

The context of the review was set by an opening discussion of the world rice economy. Rice was described as the most important food crop in the world and the major staple food of Asia's nearly 3 billion people. Asia produced about 93 percent of the total rice grown and sub-Saharan Africa less than 2 percent. Total rice production in sub-Saharan Africa was approximately the same as South Korea's and half Vietnam's. Average yields varied greatly in all regions, but yields of 6 metric tonnes per hectare (t/ha) or more were not unusual in Asia while in sub-Saharan Africa the average was 1.5 t/ha. The breakdown of CGIAR spending on rice research at the time amounted to 65.6% in Asia and 21.4% in sub-Saharan Africa (17.1% in West Africa). The facts, prima facie, hardly seemed favorable to WARDA.

The panel foresaw demand for rice rising in Asia with population growth and found the CGIAR's geographical allocations "incompatible in meeting global needs." A boost was urged in resources allocated to Asia and a corresponding decrease in investment in sub-Saharan Africa. More efficient arrangements for rice research in West Africa would have to be made. It was easy to read into this the implication that WARDA as an independent regional center would have to go.

The opportunity to respond is part of the protocol of the CGIAR review process and WARDA reacted vigorously. The stripe review was scheduled for discussion by TAC in Rome in April 1993 and would then be on the agenda at the CGIAR's midterm meeting set for May in Puerto Rico. Matlon remembers intense deadline pressure. It took time to arrive at the approach to adopt for the response and less than a week remained to prepare the final version and for Terry and Matlon to take it to Rome for the TAC meeting. The revision process continued into the weekend and a quest to print out the response and make sufficient copies required a descent into the catacombs of an all-but-deserted FAO headquarters on the Sunday evening before the Monday morning meeting. Terry and Matlon got copies to TAC members and donor representatives they thought were most open to alternative arguments and at the meeting Terry made what Matlon described as a brilliant presentation of the main points.

An endorsement of the Scobie review by TAC could have cooked WARDA's goose. Alex McCalla was in charge of preparing the TAC response to the Scobie report. Ordinarily, TAC comment on a review clearly states that the committee is largely in agreement with the findings or notes its disagreement on specific points. The TAC response referred to CGIAR strategy on rice and to certain aspects of the Scobie report but did not indicate acceptance or rejection.

Comparing Asia and Africa

Matlon says he thinks that WARDA's arguments worked because the donors were intuitively uneasy with the Scobie review's analysis, but weren't able to put their fingers on why. He says WARDA was able "to lay out the two or three or four major points using the same technique of analysis as the stripe review but turning it and adding what we thought was crucial new information." WARDA argued that the panel's analysis was incomplete. In comparing Asia and sub-Saharan Africa the review treated rice cropping cultures in the two regions as nearly identical, whereas cropping systems in Africa were much more heterogeneous and needed far more adaptive research. In addition, the environmental challenges were more severe in Africa, especially in respect to upland rice cultivation, the most prevalent type.

On the demand side, WARDA pointed out that Asian countries were producing surpluses of rice and would continue to do so for some time. West African countries on the other hand were major importers of rice. The gap between demand and rice production in sub-Saharan Africa was projected to widen and the demand for rice imports in the region to grow steadily. In contrast, the rate of increase in demand for rice was projected to fall in Asia as rising incomes enabled consumers to diversify their diets. Comparing poverty in Asia and Africa, WARDA alluded to the dynamic economies of Asia and the relatively stagnant economies of sub-Saharan Africa and pointed out that a growing percentage of Africans rely on rice as a main source of low cost calories and that this is particularly true among the urban poor.

The WARDA analysis took the stripe review's finding that the CGIAR was overinvesting in Africa and turned it on its head, suggesting, rather, that spending was disproportionately high in Asia. "There's where we said for the first time, open up, you can't just look at the CG system, look at the global system," says Matlon. WARDA noted that CGIAR spending on rice research amounted to only 4 percent of total global spending on such research. The major point was that expenditures of national research systems had been excluded from the analysis when, in fact, a number of Asian countries had strong and well financed national research programs while national systems in most sub-Saharan countries were weak and had suffered drastic declines in funding. Matlon says that the donors responded strongly to the analysis. "The donors really liked it because it sort of articulated why they felt uneasy about the Scobie analysis's conclusions."

A Special Case

WARDA and IRRI had been the subjects of regular external reviews that year and discussions of those reviews were on the agenda of the Puerto Rico meeting along with the stripe review. Both IRRI and WARDA received very positive evaluations, with WARDA getting high marks for both management and program. Terry says, this produced an "interesting situation," where the chairman of the external review, "Declan Walton was reporting very favorably on the progress of WARDA and its prospects and Scobie from the same podium was saying close the damn place down."

When the time for decision came, Matlon says that "in this open session there were 12 or 13 interventions by donors. All but one of them supported us very strongly. Each one of them took a different part of our argument and put it forward. We didn't have to present. The donors did it for us." The donor in opposition was the United States. Matlon says the U.S. representative introduced his comments by saying '"We in USAID want to make important decisions on the basis of hard analysis not emotion.' He was telling everybody else that you're just being emotional, blubber minded. It didn't go over very well at all.

TAC members seem to have accepted the Scobie panel review as an objective economic analysis, but also acknowledged the weight of other factors. This conflict is expressed in the following excerpt from a TAC statement on rice research in the CGIAR published along with the stripe review after the meeting:

> In its deliberations on the future of WARDA, TAC has faced a dilemma. The report of the Inter-Centre Review of Rice has served largely to reinforce TAC's own assessment of priorities for rice research. Consequently, if TAC applies the same rigor to rice research in West Africa which it has applied throughout its priority setting exercise, the Committee could not support a case for funding WARDA at the level required to make it a viable rice research institute.
>
> At the same time, TAC cannot escape the consequences of the policy decision taken by the CGIAR with respect to WARDA in 1986, a decision that was based on considerations in addition to priorities for rice research.

TAC acknowledged that WARDA had transformed itself into a "well-managed institute doing research of high quality." Accordingly, TAC proposed no further reduction in core funding for WARDA and stood by the expenditures allocated for the 1994 to 1998 period and the group ratified the recommendation.

Looking back on the ups and downs of the WARDA's first decade in Côte d'Ivoire, Matlon says "that system-wide study of rice was a true crisis. The rest have just been the kind of problems that all of the centers are experiencing." Now, he is able to say "I think it turned out to be the best thing for us."

A Rice Sector Study

The debate over the stripe review had shown that quantification isn't everything, but WARDA was acutely aware of how little hard data was available on which to base its plans. At the time of the stripe review, in fact, WARDA was in the process of organizing a survey of the rice sector in West Africa. Object of the new survey was to update a study coordinated by Stanford University and published in the early 1980s. Titled "Rice in West Africa," it was based on case studies of five countries and had been the first major analysis of comparative advantage in the rice market in the region.

The study's main conclusion was that rice growing was not economic in many West African countries, at least producing rice for the big coastal cities was not. Inland, domestically produced rice might be competitive with imported rice because of transportation costs. The focus was on the big cities and the study indicated that importing rice for consumption in the coastal cities was the more reasonable course.

Much had changed both in West Africa and elsewhere since the Stanford review was done. The advent of structural adjustment policies, changes in world rice prices and productivity gains in Africa all had an impact. The new study was intended to bring the analysis up to date in light of altered circumstances. The review was meant to serve as a planning tool for WARDA to focus research on the rice growing systems that appeared to have the best prospects for profitability and long-term sustainability.

WARDA lacked the staff to undertake the project, which was funded by the African Development Bank, so a contract for the job went to an American consulting firm. This special project brought Thomas Randolph to Bouaké and eventually opened the way for him to join WARDA's professional staff as a policy economist. Randolph was just completing a two-year Rockefeller postdoctoral fellowship with WARDA's irrigated rice program in Senegal and decided to take up an offer to work under contract for the consulting firm doing the rice survey. His postdoc experience in Senegal had been relevant since it involved analyzing the comparative advantage of different irrigated rice production systems in the Sahel in order to feed that information into the research planning process for those systems.

Speaking in 1996, Randolph said, "WARDA really didn't have a clue as to what was happening in the rice sector. Where was rice being produced? Which are the systems that are expanding, disappearing? The scientists themselves don't do any data collection at the regional or national level, and don't know what the trends are in terms of whether it's being grown in upland or lowland systems or irrigated systems."

Randolph collaborated on the study with another economist, David Wilcox. They had 15 months to do case studies of five countries and an overall analysis of the rice market in the region. The project was scheduled to begin in the middle of 1994, which proved very unfortunate timing. A major devaluation of the CFA franc occurred early in that year. Since gaining independence in the early 1960s, most francophone countries in the region had shared a common currency supported by the French treasury. Devaluation cut the worth of the CFA franc by half. Randolph says that the rice sector in the francophone countries was "in total chaos in this transition. Prices were going all over the place and nobody knew what the policies were going to be in the next couple of years."

The effects of devaluation subsided, but the rice study was encountering a less transient and even more serious problem, a lack of reliable data. The study was designed to cover all rice production systems so data on production costs for each system and its contribution to total production was obviously important. Also needed was information on the post-harvest costs of such things as milling, transportation and marketing. Randolph says he started out trying to collect whatever data he could get his hands on. The data simply wasn't there.

The Data Difficulty

Randolph says he thinks that the dearth of reliable data can be traced mainly to cost cutting by governments at the time of the severe budget crises of the early 1980s when data collection, such as national agricultural surveys, was among the first things to go. Since the abandonment of the surveys, says Randolph, "nobody really has a clue about what's happening on the farm or what the overall trends have been. Here in Côte d'Ivoire, if you look at the production graph after 1983 when they stopped collecting data, it's a perfect trend line. All they've done is adjust it for (growth in) rural population, absolutely no verification or corroboration of their estimates."

In 1991, a geographer as a postdoctoral project did a two-year reconnaissance survey in Côte d'Ivoire and came up with an area estimate of rice production that was half the figure FAO published. "So we're talking of orders of magnitude of give or take 100 percent," says Randolph. These statistical shortcomings apply to big producers like Côte d'Ivoire and Nigeria, which alone account for half of regional rice production. Resorting to remote sensing as a high tech alternative to country-by-country data collection might appear to be attractive, but Randolph notes that it is impractical with rainfed rice, particularly upland rice, because farmers' practice of growing several crops together makes rice production hard to estimate with any precision.

The difficulties of data gathering very early affected the character of the rice study. Initially, said Randolph, the intention was to carry out a conventional academic-style, policy-focused study, but the encounter with the realities of information gathering caused the evolution of the review into a collaborative exercise with a big training element. The aim was to create a policy analysis tool that would be applied in the same way in different countries.

The vehicle is a so-called Policy Analysis Matrix or PAM. The idea, said Randolph, is "to describe the different production systems and the production costs associated with them and then do an analysis of the financial and economic profitability of these different systems in order to get an idea of their viability, short term and long term. That information is to be fed into research planning so that we focus our research on those systems that are likely to continue and not on those likely to disappear." The key, said Randolph, is "working together with national researchers so that they will have ownership of the PAM policy-analysis tool that is created." The meeting ground was a series of training seminars supported by the World Bank and USAID.

The purpose of the rice survey was to give a clearer sense of the big picture. At the end of 1996 Randolph said, "We're still trying to sort that out because we still don't have very many of the details. It still requires lots of estimation, approximation." But enough had been learned to provide greater insight into the role of rice in West Africa's economy and to make useful comparisons with the Stanford study. The conclusions of the current review would not be radically different from those reached in the Stanford study, said Randolph. "The same general patterns of comparative advantage exist. But it's hard to make a clear comparison between their study and ours because the methodology has evolved. Also, the Stanford focus was on analyzing rice produced for the major cities whereas our analysis has been on rice produced for where it is consumed. Some of it does go to the big cities, but in most cases the cities along the coast are supplied by imported rice. Domestically produced rice is consumed either on the farm or in regional urban centers."

Transport is a big factor, says Randolph. "There's a problem when you're producing rice somewhere in the interior and transporting it to a coastal city like Abidjan or Lagos or Dakar and competing with imports there. Profitability becomes very questionable." The reverse is also true. The costs of transporting imported rice from the ports to the countryside are also punishingly high.

The Stanford report's emphasis on cities "made the results of the original study more negative than probably they should have been. Our results are more positive and they would suggest that, especially with devaluation, rice has certainly become more profitable for the different countries as an agricultural activity."

A major result of the rice study has been establishment of a rice statistics data base at WARDA. Not only is data recorded, says Randolph, "but we document how the data is estimated or collected so that researchers can judge for themselves the reliability of the data." The rice survey, therefore, not only provides encouraging evidence that rice growing in West Africa is not an economic lost cause, but also has made a start at constructing a mechanism for gathering reliable data on a regional basis where a conspicuous gap exists.

Bibliography

Adams, Adrian (1996) *A Claim to Land by the River: A Household in Senegal, 1720-1994.* Oxford University Press, New York.

Baum, Warren C. (1986) *Partners Against Hunger.* The Consultative Group on International Agricultural Research. World Bank, Washington, D.C.

Consultative Group on International Agricultural Research (1984) Report of the Second External Review of the West Africa Rice Development Association. Washington, D.C.

Consultative Group on International Agricultural Research (1993) Investment in Rice Research in the CGIAR: A Global Perspective. Report of the Inter-Centre Review of Rice. Washington, D.C.

Consultative Group on International Agricultural Research (1993) Report of the Third External Programme and Management Review of the West Africa Rice Development Association (WARDA). Washington, D.C.

Consultative Group on International Agricultural Research (2000) Report of the Fourth External Programme and Management Review of the West Africa Rice Development Association (WARDA). Washington, D.C.

Consultative Group on International Agricultural Research (2000) Charting the CGIAR's Future–Reshaping the CGIAR's Organization. Report of the Synthesis Group presented for discussion at the CGIAR's international centers week 200 in Washington, D.C.

Diemer, G. and Huibers, F.P. (1991) *Farmer managed irrigation in the Senegal Valley: Implications for the current design method.* End of Project Report, WARDA\ Wageningen Agricultural University, Water Management Project, St. Louis and Wageningen.

Dingkuhn, M., Miezan, K. (1995) Climatic determinants of irrigated rice performance in the Sahel II. Validation of photothermal constants and characterization of genotypes. *Agricultural Systems 48.*

Jamin, J.Y., Windmeijer, P.N., Thiombiano, L. (1996) The Consortium for the Sustainable Use of Inland Valley Agro-Ecosystems: A Regional Cooperation Tool Open to New Members. Paper presented at a regional workshop. WARDA. Bouaké, Côte d'Ivoire.

Jones, M.P., Dingkuhn, M., Aluko, G.K., and Semon, M. (1996) Interspecific *O. Sativa L. X. O Glaberrima* Steud. Progenies in Upland Rice Improvement. Paper. WARDA. Bouaké, Côte d'Ivoire.

Matlon, P. (1992) Collaboration Among NARS in a Regional Systems Approach: A Potential Role for International Centers. Paper presented at a SPAAR Workshop on the humid and sub-humid zones of Africa. WARDA. Bouaké, Côte d'Ivoire.

Matlon, P., Becker, M., Dingkuhn, M., Heinrichs, E., Jones, M., Miezan, K., Sahrawat, K. and Sy, A. (1995) Achievements in African Rice Research. Paper presented at Technology Development and Transfer Collaborators Workshop, Harare, Zimbabwe. WARDA. Bouaké, Côte d'Ivoire.

Matlon, P., Randolph, T. and Guei, R. (1996) Impact of Rice Research in West Africa. Paper presented at International Conference Workshop on the impact of rice research, Bangkok, Thailand. WARDA. Bouaké, Côte D'Ivoire.

West Africa Rice Development Association (1991) WARDA's Strategic Plan: 1990-2000. WARDA. Bouaké, Côte d'Ivoire.

West Africa Rice Development Association (1991) A Program of Partnership: WARDA'S New Vision and Approach to Collaboration with National Agricultural Research Systems. Bouaké, Côte d'Ivoire.

West Africa Rice Development Association (2000) The Flame Spreads into 2000: Proceedings of the Participatory Rice Improvement and Gender\User Analysis Workshop, 17-21 April 2000. Bouaké, Côte d'Ivoire.

West Africa Rice Development Association (1997) WARDA Annual Report 1996. M'be, Côte d'Ivoire.

Windmeijer, P.N. and Andriesse, W. (1993) *Inland Valleys in West Africa: an Agro-Ecological Characterization of Rice-Growing Environments*. International Institute for Land Reclamation and Improvements\ILRI, Wageningen, the Netherlands.

Index

For Product Safety Concerns and Information please contact our EU representative GPSR@taylorandfrancis.com
Taylor & Francis Verlag GmbH, Kaufingerstraße 24, 80331 München, Germany

www.ingramcontent.com/pod-product-compliance
Ingram Content Group UK Ltd.
Pitfield, Milton Keynes, MK11 3LW, UK
UKHW011018180926
475701UK00004B/815
* 9 7 8 0 3 6 7 2 4 9 6 1 8 *